CO
IN

A Perceptive Images © 2008 Publication
for Mortons Media Group Ltd

Written compiled and edited by
Keith Langston
Special thanks are due to guest
photographers David Anderson, David
Gibson, Peter Kerslake, Roger Jermy,
Brian Sharpe and John Griffith.
Also to the National Railway Museum and
Gordon Hall who facilitated
the publication of the rare 'Blue & Silver'
Princess Coronation image.
All other images, the author's collection.

Mortons Media Group
Publisher: Dan Savage
Layout and design: Lee Daniels
Production editor: Janet Richardson

Mortons Media Group Ltd
Media Centre, Morton Way,
Horncastle, Lincolnshire LN9 6JR
Tel 01507 523456

Printed by William Gibbons and Son,
Wolverhampton

Above: Double-headed Collett-inspired steam power. '5100' Class 2-6-2T 4160 outshopped by British Railways in September 1948 leads '4073' Castle Class 4-6-0 'Earl Bathurst' another Swindon product which entered GWR service in May 1936. This splendid re-creation of a BR Western region scene took place in 2007 at the West Somerset Railway. *David Gibson.*

BRITISH RAILWAYS

The steam years

If one word is used to describe the 20-year period 1948-1968 then that word should be 'change'. Not since the manic days of the 19th century railway building boom had Britain's network been subjected to so much upheaval, attracting intense political and public attention. Some simple statistics serve to illustrate the point. In 1948 the railways employed 648,740 staff, a figure that by 1960 had dramatically sunk to 514,500. Ominously the downward slide was set to continue.

As far as steam operations are concerned the figures are an even starker illustration of the changing times. On 1 January 1948 steam locomotives at work in the UK totalled just over 20,000; at the end of 1960 around 16,000 remained, but by midnight on 8 August 1968 that total was nil! Well in standard gauge terms that is; BR did continue to operate three narrow gauge steam locomotives for a little longer.

British Railways came into being on 1 January 1948, following Royal Assent being given to the Transport Act 1947. The four companies which came into being in 1923, LMS, LNER, GWR and SR became one entity with overall responsibility for the then mainly steam-operated network. The property and rolling stock of the four companies was re-branded and administratively six regions within BR were created. They were the London Midland Region, Eastern Region, North Eastern Region, Scottish Region, Southern Region and the Western Region.

To look forward it is sometimes appropriate to take a cursory glance backwards and, in the case of Britain's railways, to the events of 1939-1945. To operate for the common good, and with cohesion, the four railway companies and their subsidiary operations were placed directly under government control. The control order was made on 1 September 1939, under the Emergency Powers (Defence) Act, 1939. Official statistics collated in 1943 illustrate the enormity and complexity of the network. The 19,624 route miles when translated into single miles and counting sidings, loops etc totalled an 'actual' 59,958 miles of standard gauge track (4ft 8½ in) on which 10,300 signalboxes were controlling movements.

The number of sleepers to one mile of track was recorded as 2112. More than 1½ million cubic yards of stone ballast and several hundreds of thousands of tons of steel rails were required annually. All carriage types totalled 45,838 vehicles providing 2.65 million seats, while over 1.25 million railway wagons and 17,318

Stanier designed 8F 2-8-0 48632 is seen double heading with a BR Standard 9F 2-10-0, on a very long train of vans through the Cheshire countryside at Delamere.

containers were in service. There were some 7000 passenger stations augmented by 6900 goods stations.

Enormous tonnages of freight were carried, eg the weekly total of coal moved by the railways peaked at four million tons which was approximately 80 per cent of all that produced. The postal service was almost entirely dependent on the railways for trunk movements and over 25 million mailbags and 90 million parcels were annually moved by train. In addition to rail vehicles the companies owned approximately 35,000 horse-drawn and motor vehicles plus 130 steam ships.

Great strain was placed upon the railway system during WWII. The story of Britain's railways at war is a fascinating one and has been well documented. Many of the steam locomotives which passed into BR ownership had been used way beyond their anticipated working lives, furthermore the debilitating constraints of wartime had meant that appropriate maintenance standards were understandably difficult to achieve.

Simply put the very constituents of a working steam locomotive, if left unmaintained, will conspire to produce impaired performance, or at worst failure. Water, steam, high temperature combustible gases, various metals both ferrous and non-ferrous and reciprocating motion are not naturally compatible bedfellows. Thus British Railways inherited a large amount of rolling stock, and indeed items of infrastructure, which in 21st century terms were less than fit for purpose. The post-war government considered that something had to be done, that something in their view was the creation of British Railways in 1948; that organisation would continue to operate steam locomotives albeit in decreasing numbers for 20 years.

BR continued to build (or buy from outside contractors) steam locomotives from the programmes already in place by the big four, in addition to building locomotives in their own right.

4 March 1967 ex-GWR 4-6-0 Castle Class 4079 'Pendennis Castle' is pictured on Gresford Bank with the return leg of The Birkenhead Flyer Didcot-Chester-Didcot railtour. Locomotive 4079 was preserved and went to work in Australia, the loco is now back in the UK.

Steam classes built by BR included '4073' Class 4-6-0 Castles, '6959' Class 4-6-0 Halls and 4-6-0 '78xx' Class Manors, '15xx' Class 0-6-0PT, '16xx' Class 0-6-0PT, '5101' Class 2-6-2T, '57xx' Class 0-6-0PT ex-Great Western Railway designs.

West Country/Battle of Britain and Merchant Navy Class 4-6-2 ex-Southern Railway designs.

Ivatt modified '8P' Princess Coronation Class 4-6-2, Stanier '5MT' Class 4-6-0 Black Five, '2MT' Class 2-6-2, '4MT' Class 2-6-4T, '4MT' 2-6-0, '2MT' Class 2-6-0 ex-London Midland & Scottish designs.

Peppercorn 'A1' Class 4-6-2 and 'A2' Class 4-6-2, 'J72' Class 0-6-0T, 'B1' Class 4-6-0, 'K1' Class 4-6-0 ex-London North Eastern Railway designs.

Even though modernisation was very much the order of the day the newly formed British Railways made a decision to continue building steam locomotives and embarked upon a programme of design and build under the leadership of Robert Riddles. Those locomotive classes were generally termed BR Standard Designs. The first Standard locomotive rolled out of

the workshops in 1951 and the last in 1959. In addition BR took into stock ex-War Department 2-8-0, 2-10-0 and 0-6-0ST Austerity locomotives.

As the railway workers of 1948 considered their futures within the new organisation, and in many cases lamented the demise of the old companies, they could have been excused for thinking that the major change to their working lives had already taken place. They were to be proved wrong as the creation of BR was only the start. The eyes of politicians, and others with vested interests were focussed on the railways; they would not avert them for some time to come.

The first decade of BR's reign also saw the continued introduction of diesel and electric traction and naturally changes in working practices. Office and managerial staff were not insulated from change, and as the company began to computerise, job losses naturally followed. Traditionally railway workers' wages tended to be below those of employees in other industries. Unrest over pay began to gather momentum. In the December of 1953 both railway unions, ASLEF

In this delightful period study Britannia Class 4-6-2 70025 'Western Star' is pictured at Carlisle in September 1967. The loco is preparing to leave the train having worked the 3.15pm Crewe-Carlisle service. *Roger Jermy.*

(Associated Society of Locomotive Engineers and Firemen) and the NUR (National Union of Railwaymen) threatened strike action, it was only averted at the last minute.

That unrest did not go away and ASLEF members took action from 28 May to 13 June 1955, the first national stoppage on the railways since the 1926 General Strike. However they did so without the support of their colleagues who were members of the NUR, whose officials instructed them to work normally. The action caused bad feelings between men who had been close workmates; in the heat of strike action and picket activity many hurtful things were said. The wounds inflicted would be long remembered.

Change continued to take place and the 1950s Modernisation Plan introduced under the auspices of The British Transport Commission was judged with the benefit of hindsight as being a failure. The famous English Electric Deltic locomotive was introduced in 1955 but in general a great deal of money was invested in what turned out to be mainly unproven replacement diesel traction. The plan also failed to tackle restrictive work practices and did nothing to stop railway freight business transferring to road haulage. In 1954 the Woodhead Route, which was Britain's first fully operational inter-city overhead electric main line, came into being; it represented yet another nail in the steam coffin.

The failure of the Modernisation Plan soured the relationship between railway and government for decades. The British Transport Commission continued to look for solutions to the problems of the network; their chosen way was the appointment in June 1961 of

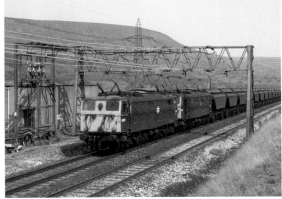

Originally opened in 1845 the Manchester-Sheffield 'Woodhead' line was reopened as a 1500v DC electrified route in 1954. Through passenger services were withdrawn in 1970 and in 1981 the Woodhead Tunnel was closed and the electric locomotives withdrawn, one example was preserved.

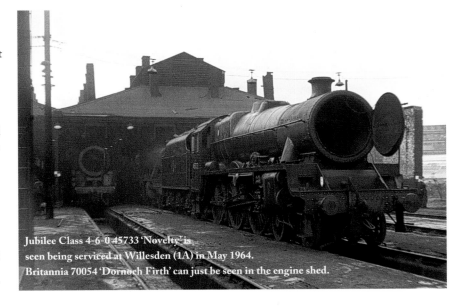

Jubilee Class 4-6-0 45733 'Novelty' is seen being serviced at Willesden (1A) in May 1964. Britannia 70054 'Dornoch Firth' can just be seen in the engine shed.

Princess Coronation Class 8P 4-6-2 46240 'City of Coventry' is seen 'on shed' at Willesden.

BR Standard 2-6-0 4MT Class, pictured between turns in March 1965.

The crew of ex-LNER Class 04/8 2-8-0 pose on the veranda of the signalbox to have their picture taken with the 'Bobby' at Scrosby in 1963.

Dr Richard Beeching. In the first instance Beeching was chairman of the BTC for the last six months of that organisation's life and then chairman of a newly constituted British Railways Board. Beeching was an industrial high flyer who had been tipped as a future chairman of Imperial Chemical Industries.

He took up his new position on a salary of £24,000 a year making him Britain's highest-paid civil servant. Dr Beeching immediately created his own team comprising of railway men and incomers; he got straight to work although some would prefer the term 'began sharpening his axe!' He was targeted with halting loss making within BR and planning for the future. His team conducted network-wide surveys into goods and passengers carried against costs incurred. From the early days of his tenure it became obvious that Beeching believed that the railways were

The driver of Light Pacific 4-6-2 34037 'Clovelly' looks thoughtfully back along his train. Respected railwayman and author RNH Hardy summed up the steam footplate relationship with this wonderful quotation. "Everything depended on the ability and temperament of two men charged with a great responsibility, working together to find steam and power, to run to time and in complete safety."

doing much which could be done more economically by road transport.

In March 1963 Beeching presented his first report, it was a 140-page document entitled The Reshaping of British Railways. Controversial hardly described his findings and the resultant shock waves went through the whole railway industry and the British public. 'He will never get away with it' was a phrase uttered by many within the industry and even some in parliament. But in the main he did; his team also produced more details in a second report published in February 1965.

Among Beeching's findings, half of the network's stations produced only two per cent of the traffic, approximately 1/3rd of the track mileage carried in ton or passenger miles only one per cent of the overall total, and staggeringly out of 18,500 main line passenger carriages only 5500 were in year-round daily

And then there were none; a line-up of ex-GWR locomotives, waiting for the cutter's torch at Woodham Brothers' Barry scrapyard. According to the painted warning, the loco nearest the camera was reserved for presentation; sadly it did not make it.

Ex-Caledonian Railway (then LMS) Pickersgill 1916-built 4-4-0 3P 54461 is seen in BR ownership with a train of 'lifted' railway sleepers at Strawfrank Junction, Carstairs. Note the fireman looking back to make sure that the train safely negotiates the set of points. This locomotive was withdrawn from service in 1959. *David Anderson.*

service. The findings were welcomed by the then Tory Minister of Transport who described it as 'a superb effort'. The minister was Ernest Marples (later Sir and then Lord) He was also the owner of Marples Ridgeway, a road construction company. When it was pointed out to him that being transport minister did not sit well with his company's activities he simply transferred his financial interest in the firm to his wife!

Beeching left his BRB post in May 1965. Steam traction on BR was set to continue for another three years and two months. Not all of the 'Doctor's' proposals were immediately acted upon, but the die was cast and Britain's rail network would never be the same again. In 1948 there were 19,630 route miles, by 1960 the total was reduced to 18,565 and by 1969 (one year after the end of steam) the total was recorded as being only 13,261 miles. The report can be credited with encouraging further development of the Inter-City passenger services and the introduction of 'liner' freight train service. ■

Inside the 'round house' at Willesden 1A motive power depot. Centre of the picture is Royal Scot Class 4-6-0 46119 'Lancashire Fusilier'.

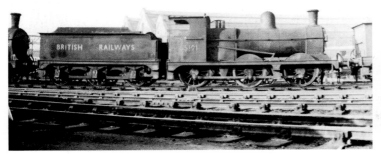

Ex-LNER 0-6-0 'J10' Class 65191 is seen at Gorton in 1954 with the earliest British Railways insignia on the tender.

Still in LMS livery but with a BR number, ex LMS 4-4-0 3 Cylinder Compound 4P is pictured at Heaton Mersey (9F) in October 1951.

Above 'Scottish Director' D11/2 Class 3P 4-4-0 62691 'Laird of Balmawhapple' is pictured passing Dalmeny Station in 1955. *Below* Hughes/Fowler 'Crab' 2-6-0 5MT 42740 is seen at Barassie Station with an Ayr-bound freight in 1951. *Both images David Anderson.*

THE LOCOMOTIVE
BUILDERS
Oliver Vaughan Snell Bulleid

Ex-Southern Region Bulleid-designed locomotives could be seen in the service of British Railways all over their home territory, and some even survived right up until 9 July 1967, the date of the end of steam on the Southern. Bulleid designs accounted for 180 of the 1838 ex-SR steam locomotives which ran in revenue-earning service for British Railways after nationalisation. He was responsible for two similar looking air smoothed casing 4-6-2 Pacific designs and one very functional, but strange looking, 0-6-0 freight locomotive. No less than 32 Bulleid locomotives survived the end of steam on BR and are preserved, many in operational condition.

Bulleid (1882-1970) was born in Invercargill, New Zealand, on 19 September 1882 but his family later moved to the UK, and his formal education was undertaken at Accrington Technical School in Lancashire. His introduction to locomotive engineering was with the Great Northern Railway; he joined their Doncaster Works as an apprentice in 1901 and entered their employ 'proper' in 1906. In 1908 Bullied went to France to work as Chief Draughtsman, and then Assistant Works Manager, for the French Westinghouse Company. He then had a three-year spell with the UK Board of Trade as Chief Mechanical and Electrical Engineer for British Exhibits.

In 1912 he began his employment with the North Eastern Railway as Principal Assistant to the great NH Gresley. In 1923 'grouping' saw the GNR become the London & North Eastern Railway; following that change Bullied continued to serve under Gresley in the same role. Thus he clocked up a total of 22 years working with the man whose name became synonymous with the successful streamlining of steam locomotives. Bulleid was renowned for his flair and innovation and put both facets to good use at the LNER during the design and building of the streamlined 'Silver Jubilee' coaches.

In September 1937 Bulleid joined the Southern Railway and began working alongside his predecessor REL Maunsell. His first few years in post were spent working on design improvements with locomotives of the existing SR fleet. When, in 1939, the Southern Railway board identified their urgent need for a new fast heavy passenger locomotive they turned to their new Chief Mechanical Engineer.

His original proposals were for locomotives in the 4-8-0, 4-8-2 and 2-6-2 configuration ideas which did not find favour with the board in general and the railway's civil engineer in particular. Bulleid therefore turned his

Left: **No less than 32 Bulleid locomotives made it into preservation. This is one of them, Merchant Navy Class 8P 4-6-2 Pacific 35005 Canadian Pacific, which was originally fitted with a mechanical stoker. Pictured during a 2006 visit to the Churnet Valley Railway.** *David Gibson.*

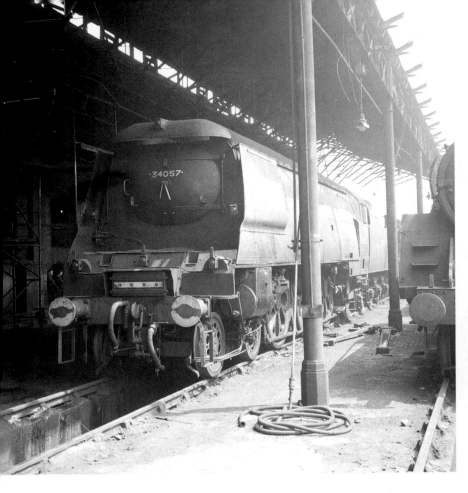

The ungainly looking 0-6-0 Q1 Class 33016 is seen taking water in this late 1950s image.

This study of 35003 'Royal Mail' shows clearly the detail of the strong but lightweight 'boxpok' wheels.

Under cover, well almost! Battle of Britain Class 34057 'Biggin Hill' seen at Nine Elms. This locomotive was cut up for scrap in 1967.

Pictured on the turntable at Nine Elms (70A) is BB Class 34077 '603 Squadron', a BR built member of the class. Post 1948 BR continued to build Bulleid Pacifics. At that time Nine Elms had an allocation of 17 Light Pacifics and 12 Merchant Navy Class engines. Stewarts Lane (72A) had the largest total allocation, 28 BB and 8 MN class.

attention to designing a 4-6-2 Pacific type with a lighter axle loading; that project received the blessing of his directors. However final design and building was slowed down by the onset of WWII but Bulleid did gain permission to commence building the first 10 of his unique Merchant Navy Class 8P 4-6-2 Pacifics. The first example of his revolutionary design was rolled out of Eastleigh Works in February 1941. Innovation was very much the Bulleid way and much has been written about the originality of his designs which included streamlining the SR called Air Smoothed Casing, chain driven valve gear immersed in an oil bath, American style 'boxpok' type wheels, electric lighting and an all-welded construction steel (not copper) firebox.

In theory the 'oil bath' should have been a maintenance fitter's dream but in fact it caused a great many more problems than it solved. The steel fireboxes had a less than satisfactory service life with the first 10 all being replaced after only seven years. On the credit side the class were a whole lot better performers than

any other SR express passenger locomotives of the time and importantly the Merchant Navies greatly reduced 'hammer blow' (and therefore track damage).
The type was very popular with locomotive crews but not universally so with maintenance departments.

The Southern Railway also needed an express locomotive with greater route availability and to fulfil that need Bulleid designed a 'scaled down' version of those first air smoothed Pacifics, that type became the West Country, Battle of Britain Class 7P5F 4-6-2. British Railways continued with the Merchant Navy Class 8P 4-6-2 building programme at the ex-SR Eastleigh Works and turned out the last of that class in 1949. The Merchant Navy class totalled 30 engines. The smaller and less powerful Bulleid Pacifics, which comprised the 110 members of the West Country, Battle of Britain Class 7P5F 4-6-2, were built at both Brighton and Eastleigh works, between 1945 and 1947 under the SR, and from 1948 to 1951 by BR.

Locomotives of both classes of Bulleid Pacific were extensively rebuilt under British Railways. The Merchant Navy class were all rebuilt between 1956 and 1959. The rebuilding of 60 of the lighter Pacifics was also decided upon and that project got under way in 1957. Essentially the rebuilding centred on the removal of the 'air smoothed casing' and the replacement of the chain driven valve gear with more conventional equipment. Square smoke deflectors were added and many observers have since commented upon the similarity in looks between the rebuilt Bulleid locomotives and the BR Standard Pacifics.

During BR steam days Bulleid's only freight locomotive design continued to serve the Southern

Unrebuilt Bulleid Light Pacific 34023 'Blackmore Vale' waits to exit Waterloo Station, after the stock of its train had been removed by the station pilot loco. Blackmore Vale entered Southern Railway service in February 1946 and was given the SR number 21C123; taken into BR stock it was allocated the number 34023 in April 1948. Withdrawn in 1967 it is a preserved engine.

Region. The strange looking 0-6-0 Q1 Class was a much revered engine and some commentators have even used the words 'brilliant' and 'outstanding' to describe the powerful inside-cylinder machines. Richard Maunsell had introduced his Q design 0-6-0 in 1938 and that loco had proved its worth, but lacked the power needed for the increased freight traffic brought about by WWII. Bulleid's Q1 development was an extremely powerful engine which carried a 5F power classification; importantly it enjoyed total route availability on the Southern. Built at Ashford and Brighton works in 1942 the 40-strong class served both the Southern and BR well with three of the class staying in service until January 1966.

After nationalisation Oliver Bulleid, who in 1949 was awarded a CBE, went to work for British Railways as Chief Mechanical Engineer of BR Southern Region, but the relationship was short lived. He resigned from BR later that year and took up the post of Consultant Engineer (later becoming CME) with CIE, the Irish State Railways. While there, in addition to experimenting with a turf (peat) burning steam locomotive, he actually presided over the phasing out of steam traction, and oversaw the introduction of diesel traction. Bulleid retired in 1958 and went to live in Devon, he later moved to Malta where he died on 25 April 1970. ■

Almost the end, unrebuilt West Country Class 4-6-2 34004 'Yeovil' pictured in Eastleigh locomotive shed alongside an unidentified Standard Tank; both looking forlorn and unloved. It was just a week before the end of steam on the Southern Region and 34004 would eventually meet with the cutter's torch at John Cashmore's yard, Newport, in October 1967. *Roger Jermy.*

Battle of Britain Class 4-6-2 34086 '219 Squadron' pictured at the buffer stops, Waterloo in 1964. Note the destination board on the platform. This locomotive entered service in December 1948 and therefore spent all of its life in British Railways' ownership. It was withdrawn in June 1966 and cut up in the October of that year.

BULLEID DESIGNED **PACIFICS**

Above: **Merchant Navy Class 8** **4-6-2 Pacific 35005 'Canadian Pacific' in unrebuilt form is pictured at Waterloo Station in 1956, waiting to depart with a train for Exeter. 35005 entered service in December 1941 and was rebuilt in May 1959. It was withdrawn from service in October 1965 having travelled approx 975,000 miles. 'Canadian Pacific' is a preserved locomotive.**

Left: **Merchant Navy Class 8** **4-6-2 Pacific 35028 'Clan Line' in rebuilt form is also pictured at London's Waterloo Station awaiting to depart with a Bournemouth train in 1960. 35028 entered service in December 1948 and was rebuilt in October 1958. It was withdrawn from service in July 1967 having travelled over 790,000 miles. 'Clan Line' is a preserved locomotive.**

West Country, Battle of Britain Class 7P5F 4-6-2s both pictured from slightly different angles in October 1965, the location is Southampton Central.

Right: Unrebuilt example 34002 'Salisbury' entered service in May 1945 and never having been rebuilt was withdrawn in April 1967. Note the fireman on top of the tender, straightening out the coal as the loco takes water.

Below: Rebuilt example 34013 'Okehampton' entered service in October 1945, and was rebuilt in October 1957 and withdrawn in July 1967.

SAME LOCATION, DIFFERENT DAY...

British S

THE LAST STEAM-HAULED
STATE FUNERAL

During the winter of 2002 the television viewers of the UK were invited to vote for the person they considered to be the 'Greatest Briton'. At the end of the occasionally controversial four-week-long series the Right Honourable Sir Winston Leonard Spencer Churchill KG OM CH TD FRS PC (Can) was pronounced the popular winner.

Former Northern Ireland Secretary the late Dr Mo Mowlam put the case for Churchill. Summarising her argument, she said: "If Britain, its eccentricity, its big heartedness, its strength of character, has to be summed up in one person, it has to be Winston Churchill." Worthy of note is that in second place, only some 60,000 votes behind, was the great railway engineer Isambard Kingdom Brunel.

On 30 January 1965 the celebrated wartime leader made his final journey, partially courtesy of British Railways. A hand picked locomotive footplate crew from the 'top link' at Nine Elms motive power depot (70A) were called upon to be in charge of the locomotive. Fittingly Bulleid Light Pacific 4-6-2 34051 'Winston Churchill' was chosen to haul the special train from London Waterloo to Handborough in Oxfordshire, it being the station nearest to St Martin's Church, Bladon where the world renowned statesman was laid to rest.

Queen Elizabeth II had decreed that the occasion be a 'State Funeral', the first for a non-royal family member for over 50 years. After a service at St Paul's Cathedral the coffin was first carried down the Thames by launch and then transferred to the waiting train at Waterloo's Platform 11. During the journey down river there had been a fly-past of RAF jets and a 19-gun salute.

On arrival at Waterloo the responsibility passed to the staff of British Railways in particular and to the Nine Elms engine crew, Driver Alf (Lou) Hurley, Fireman James (Jim) Lester, and Chief Inspector Bill Neal in particular. The train consisted of five Pullman cars and a bogie van containing the coffin, all under the watchful eye of Royal Train Guard Mr WH Horwill.

The then home shed of 34051 was 72B Salisbury where the loco was at that time stored out of use (but not condemned). After being selected for the special task the 1946-built Battle of Britain Class engine was moved to Nine Elms shed for cleaning and preparation. As was standard practice on such occasions a reserve locomotive was selected and similarly prepared. That engine was 4-6-2 Battle of Britain Class 34064 'Fighter Command' which was, on the day, stood in readiness in the 'Down Loop' at Staines Central. 'She' was not needed. The funeral train had to pass from, what was to the crew, familiar Southern Region territory into ex-GWR unfamiliar territory, and so prior to the event the Nine Elms men had made a route-learning trip aboard a Diesel Multiple Unit.

Left: **Churchill's funeral train pictured near Didcot North Junction, en route to Bladon.** *David Anderson.*

In deference to the 'Great Man' three pristine white discs from the special Southern headcode 'four set' reserved for the Royal Train were used, and fixed so as to represent the famous Churchillian 'V' for victory sign. Observers noted that the disks were so placed on the tender of the locomotive as it approached Platform 11 and that they were then transferred to the front of the engine after 'she' had backed onto the train. The three-disc headcode was normally associated with breakdown trains.

At 13:28 with no whistles sounding the last BR steam-hauled state funeral train smoothly and solemnly departed from Waterloo, following a green flag signal from Mr Horwill. History has recorded that members of the public stood head bowed as the train passed by and that all along the route ex-military personnel in

4-6-2 Battle of Britain Class 34064 'Fighter Command' the selected reserve engine in full cry passing Raynes Park in 1960.

uniforms gave Sir Winston their last salute. Locomotive number 34051 is preserved in the care of the National Railway Museum, sister engine 34064 was cut up in October 1966.

Soon after the funeral a story started to circulate which although fanciful in the extreme is worthy of the telling. The tale goes that Sir Winston, being a man who left nothing to chance, had a big hand in the pre-planning of his funeral. In doing so he reportedly met with a senior British Railways official who respectfully suggested to him that Waterloo would not be the easiest station at which to transfer his cortege from the river Thames to a train. The story goes that the redoubtable Winston looking the official straight in the eye said: "If General de Gaulle dies before me you can start the train from anywhere you like, but if I go first I leave from Waterloo!" Sir Winston, it seemed, relished the thought of de Gaulle standing uncomfortably at Waterloo. ■

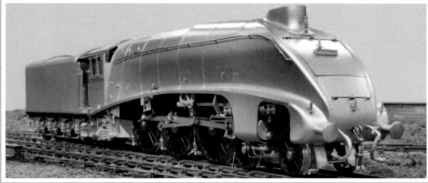
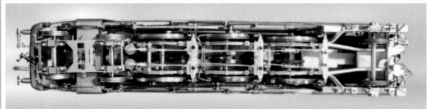

British Steam

The Southern Region of British Railways, created in 1948, was the successor of the Southern Railway, which itself was a creation born of the 1923 railway amalgamations. At that time the separate companies operating in the region were joined together to form one entity. The principal separate companies were London & South Western Railway, London Brighton & South Coast Railway, South Eastern Railway, London Chatham & Dover Railway and the South Eastern & Chatham Railway.

W hen the Southern Region of BR came into being, it inherited some 1856 steam locomotives from the Southern Railway, many of which had been operated by the original companies. The Southern, more than any other region at that time was heavily electrified, but nevertheless steam still played a very important role. Although other ex-SR locomotive works ceased to be of major operational importance under British Railways, Brighton and Eastleigh works survived and to a degree even flourished. Brighton Works played a big part in the production of BR Standard Locomotives, and both works continued to build SR Bulleid designs in the early BR days.

Brighton works opened in 1848 initially to serve the LB&SCR. After amalgamation the works went into a

Below: **Preserved N15 Class 30777 Sir Lamiel is seen in preservation, during a main line run at Delamere on the old Cheshire Lines Conference.**

Immaculate in Southern Railway livery V (Schools) Class 5P 4-4-0 30928 'Stowe'.

steady decline but the advent of WWII meant that manufacturing capacity was urgently needed, as a result the works was then modernised and refitted. The last member of the Bulleid Light Pacific BB Class 34110 '66 Squadron' left the works in January 1951. The last 'batch' of steam locomotives to be turned out of the works were BR 2-6-4T Class 4 mixed traffic locomotives numbered 80145 to 80154, which were outshopped between 1954 and 1956.

Eastleigh had two railway associated works, a carriage and wagon works which first began building railway vehicles in 1889, and a locomotive works which opened in 1909, both were operated by the L&SWR. After nationalisation, Eastleigh Locomotive Works continued to complete orders for steam locomotives in addition to being utilised in the refurbishment of EMU stock. The last Bulleid Merchant Navy Class 4-6-2 Pacific built at Eastleigh was 35030 'Elder Dempster Lines' rolled out in April 1949. All the work carried out by Ashford Works (which was opened in 1847) was transferred to Eastleigh in 1962. The events of railway rationalisation carried out in the 1960s saw the carriage and wagon works close, despite a great deal of local protest.

For operational purposes the old Southern Railway was split into Western and Eastern sections, a practice which continued under BR. In addition the Southern Region was responsible for the Isle of Wight Railways as was its predecessor. At the onset of BR there were 37 steam motive power depots in the Southern Region the principal ones being Nine Elms (70A), Eastleigh (71A), Exmouth Junction (72A), Stewarts Lane (73A), Ashford (74A) and Brighton (75A).

In addition to his own designs Bulleid oversaw a great number of modifications and rebuilds to steam locomotives designed by his predecessors. Two of which were Robert Urie who served the L&SWR between 1912 and 1922 and Richard Edward Lloyd Maunsell who served the Southern Railway between 1923 and 1937. Locomotives produced under the reign of those two engineers made up a large proportion of those taken into BR stock in 1948.

Above: **Pictured in 1958 at Exeter Central is 30333 H15 Class 4-6-0 Maunsell rebuild of a Drummond engine.**

Top: **Schools Class 4-4-0 30905 'Tonbridge' is pictured on the turntable at Nine Elms (70A) in 1959.**

Class U 2-6-0 (Mogul) is seen having just been lit up on shed at Yeovil (72C).

There were others from a bygone age whose creations, having more than stood the test of time, were still steaming in 1948: Dugald Drummond L&SWR 1895 to 1912, H Wainwright 1899 to 1913, SE&CR, LB Billington LB&SC 1911 to 1922. Robert Urie is perhaps best remembered for his S15 Class 4-6-0 goods locomotives and his N15 Class of passenger engines, of which Maunsell rebuild 30777 'Sir Lamiel' is now a part of the National Collection.

Maunsell designed the V (Schools) Class 5P 4-4-0s which were acclaimed as being the most powerful locomotives of that wheel arrangement ever built for Britain's railways; 40 of them were built at Eastleigh Works between 1930 and 1935, they were originally intended to work on the Hastings route, all survived to run in BR livery. In addition Maunsell rebuilt the 74 Urie N15 Class King Arthur 4-6-0s, all of which passed into BR stock.

End of the road. 31900 U1 2-6-0 Mogul awaits the cutting torch. Stored out of use Redhill (75B) 1963.

His other notable passenger locomotive class was the Lord Nelson LN Class and 16 of the 4-6-0s were built in 1926. They gained a reputation among enginemen for being 'moody' ie a loco which on one day steamed freely would struggle for no apparent reason on another! But they were impressive machines, and thankfully 30850 'Lord Nelson' survived into preservation.

Waterloo Station is perhaps the London terminus most people associate with the Southern Railway and thus the Southern Region of British Railways, but Victoria, Cannon Street and Charing Cross all have strong historic links with Southern services. At the time of nationalisation SR had the highest density of electrified lines which together with London Underground handled the majority of the capital's commuter services. It is worthy of note that in addition to normal safety procedures the enginemen and operational railway workers on the Southern had to be constantly aware of the added danger of the electrified '3rd' rail.

Urie-designed Hump Shunter 30495 G16 Class 4-8-0T 7F, which dates from 1921, is seen at Feltham.

Line-up of Class W 2-6-4T locos at Feltham, 31912 at the front of the row.

Maunsell Lord Nelson 4-6-0 30857 'Lord Howe' is seen at Bournemouth.

British Steam

30241 at Waterloo, Drummond, 0-4-4T M7 Motor Tank

30040 at Bournemouth, Drummond, 0-4-4T M7 Motor Tank

D1 Class 4-4-0 2P, Maunsell rebuild of a Wainwright locomotive.

Among the express passenger services on the region were boat trains from the capital to Southampton as the famous south coast docks were then still handling a large volume of Atlantic Ocean liner traffic. Such trains would almost always have an extra baggage car included in order to accommodate the high volume of luggage usually associated with sea travel. In addition Folkestone Harbour Station was regularly served by boat trains and there were also intensive services to Dover.

During the period of WWII the tracks of the 'Southern' were among the busiest in Britain with special freight and troop trains, especially at the time of the Dunkirk evacuations and the subsequent allied invasion of mainland Europe. But in general terms the SR was not regarded as a high volume freight carrier and that fact is reflected in the locomotive types operated by both the SR and their successor the SR of BR. There was however a reasonable level of freight traffic generated by the collieries in Kent and the docks at Southampton, Folkestone and of course Dover.

A speciality of the Southampton freight trains was the conveyance from the docks of bananas which had arrived in the UK by custom built fast ships.

Among the towns and cities served by the SR were Bournemouth and Weymouth, Brighton, Eastbourne and Hastings, Portsmouth and Worthing, Ashford, Canterbury and Margate, Woking, Basingstoke, Salisbury, Yeovil and Exeter. Many of the secondary and branch lines in the region were included in the Beeching Report and suffered reduced services or total closure. ■

Urie Class S15 4-6-0 6F is seen between turns at Nine Elms in 1959.

Black smoke indicates that the fireman of ex-LNER K3/2 2-6-0 (Mogul) number 61991 is still 'bending his back' as the locomotive powers its freight train off the Jamestown Viaduct in May 1956.

LOCOMOTIVE FIREMEN AT WORK

Locomotive firemen will have joined the steam shed (motive power depot) as cleaners where in the dirt and grime they would have learnt the rudiments of steam locomotive preparation and disposal. After attaining a predetermined level of competence they would be promoted to 'passed cleaner' in order to perform some minor firing roles around the yard, and then eventually promoted to 'locomotive fireman'. The role of a steam locomotive fireman can be described as 'boiler manager' charged with providing the driver with all the steam needed to perform the task in hand, and preferably no more! Excessive plumes of steam from the loco's safety valves represent wasted energy. The final step to becoming a driver is 'past fireman'.

This superb 1960s study of ex-LMS Jubilee Class 4-6-0 number 45718 'Dreadnought' speeding along the West Coast Main Line near Thankerton clearly shows the fireman perfectly balanced and about his work; the smoke is starting to turn darker.

Both images
David Anderson.

British Steam

The driver of the 'down' Royal Scot is seen framed in the cab window as he eases his train along the West Coast Main Line at Elvanfoot. The perfect express lines of the ex-LMS Stanier 4-6-2 Pacific Princess Coronation Class number 46240 'City of Coventry' are shown to perfection.

LOCOMOTIVE DRIVERS AT WORK

All steam drivers would have served as firemen before attaining that rank. During their career drivers would be constantly gaining extra knowledge. As work rosters changed new routes had to be learnt and that included knowing the position of the signals, gradients, water towers or troughs, junctions and points etc. Before taking a train over what to them was a new route drivers would be asked to 'sign for it' thereby confirming that they were 'past out' to take a train along it. In addition drivers needed to have familiarity with any locomotive type they may be called upon to drive. Given the type of home shed they were attached to that could be several types, which may have vastly different power classifications.

By comparison the austere shape of Riddles Class WD 8F 2-8-0 number 90513 looks a little ungainly as it trundles its heavy train of vans along the Edinburgh Suburban Line at Blackford Hill, note the driver watching the 'road'. However both locomotives represent the epitome of steam locomotive design. The engines are perfect for the task at hand, with both drivers equal masters of their craft.

Both images David Anderson.

STEAM ON THE ISLE OF WIGHT

The railways of the Isle of Wight had since amalgamation been part of the Southern Railway and so in January 1948 they also became part of British Railways, and for administrative reasons they became an element of the Southern Region of BR. There were no less than 27 steam locomotives allocated to the island's railways at that time and the main motive power depot Ryde, boasted the Southern Region shed code of 71F.

Taking water at Ventnor is Class 02 4-4-0T locomotive 26 'Whitwell'.

The island's locomotives were all of Southern Railway origin but did not carry numbers in the Southern sequence and were given single and double digit numbers of their own, ranging from one to 34 with gaps created by scrapping. All of the Isle of Wight engines were named after locations on the island.

In the aging fleet BR inherited, were four members of the 'E1' 0-6-0T Class 2F, a Stroudley design for the London Brighton & South Coast Railway dating from 1874-91, which were referred to on the Southern as 'Black Tanks'. They carried the numbers 1 to 4.

There were two members of the 'AIX' 0-6-0T Class 0P known as 'Terriers'. These diminutive locomotives were another Stroudley design for the LB&SC and dating originally from 1872 were rebuilt in 1911. The 'Terriers' carried the numbers 8 and 13.

The most prolific class of steam locomotives allocated to the IoW was the 'O2' 0-4-4T 1P; originally dating from 1889 they were an Adams design for the London & South Western Railway and were given a 1P power rating. There were 21 allocated and they carried the consecutive numbers 14 to 34.

Above and right: **Class 02s 14 'Fishbourne' and 24 'Calbourne' are seen on the Locomotive Club of Great Britain, Vectis Farewell Tour which took place on 3 October 1965. Vectis was the name given to the island by the Romans.**

Under BR ownership the main focus of activity on the Isle of Wight railways was closure. At the onset there were steam-operated routes between Ryde and Ventnor, Ryde and Cowes, Newport and Freshwater, Merstone and Ventnor (two stations) and Brading and Bembridge. Effectively the island was served with a north-south service and interconnecting east-west services. There was even a semi-fast named train 'The Tourist' which ran from Ventnor (Town) to Sandown and then via Merstone to Newport where it reversed, and then continued on to Freshwater. The end of steam was a gradual process as various sections were closed. The final end came courtesy of Dr Beeching in 1966. ■

All of the island's steam locomotives were named and BR carried on that tradition.

FISHBOURNE

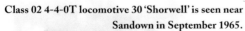

Class 02 4-4-0T locomotive 30 'Shorwell' is seen near Sandown in September 1965.

Locomotives 32 'Chale' and 20 'Shanklin', both class 02 4-4-0T, are seen on shed at Ryde (71F) in October 1965.

LIST OF CLOSURES UNDER BR:

Merstone-Ventnor 15 September 1953
Brading-Bembridge 21 September 1963
Newport-Freshwater 21 September 1953
Ryde-Cowes 6 February 1966
Shanklin-Ventnor (section of Ryde-Ventnor) 18 April 1966

THE LOCOMOTIVE
BUILDERS
Charles Benjamin Collett

Highlighting some of the achievements of the Great Western Railway locomotive engineer CB
Collett (1871-1952) does not lessen the importance of the contributions made to steam
locomotive development by those GWR chief engineers who immediately preceded or succeeded
him. It is a generally held belief that Collett (GWR Chief Mechanical Engineer 1922-1941) was
an 'improver' of the designs attributed to his predecessor George Jackson Churchward, and many
considered Churchward to be the greatest GWR locomotive builder.

During the period of BR steam on the 'Western' (1948-1965) the biggest number of locomotives from any single designer/improver, and thus the most widely remembered were those of CB Collett. British Railways inherited some 2288 locomotives which can be directly attributed to Collett, almost 60 per cent of the GWR total.

Collett's successor, Frederick William Hawksworth was only in post for six years before the advent of British Railways, but the designs and developments he was associated with were all regarded as fine engines.

Collett was born in 1871 and after his formal education at Merchant Taylors' School, London and the City and Guilds College he went to work for Maudslay, Sons & Field Ltd as an engineering pupil. He entered the hallowed portals of Swindon Works for the first time in 1893. He worked his way up from Junior Draughtsman to CME via Technical Inspector and Works Manager; his colleagues at the time included one William A Stanier.

He became Churchward's heir apparent in 1919 when appointed to the post of Assistant CME having by that time spent 20 years in senior positions. He became Chief Mechanical Engineer of the GWR in 1922, after Churchward retired. Tragedy struck in 1923 when his wife became seriously ill and unexpectedly died. Always a private man, thereafter he became even more so, and rarely if ever attended works social functions. Collett

never chose to work with other railway companies thus clocking up an amazing total of 48 years at Swindon Works; he retired in 1941 when in his 70th year.

He was awarded the OBE for his work on munitions manufacturing processes during WWI and served the town of Swindon as a Justice of the Peace from 1921 to 1928. His retirement took him to London where he died aged 81, 5 April 1952. Other retired GWR personnel were known to regularly visit the works, not so Collett, he virtually severed all links with the company he had served so loyally.

The GWR locomotive fleet taken into stock by BR was all the better for Collett's influence. Although most commentators pulled up short of calling Collett personally a great designer, all acknowledged his superb engineering and organisational skills. In line with most CMEs he did not necessarily hold the pencil that turned the ideas into steam locomotive designs, but he firmly controlled the team that did. The BR era in the Western Region was dominated by Collett engines and they weren't all express passenger types. In fact the pannier tanks, from five separate classes originated by him, totalled 997 locomotives. Horses, as they say for courses, the WR had a lot of work which suited Pannier Tanks.

Collett's first big impact on the GWR was the introduction of his 4073 'Castle' Class 7P 4-6-0 locomotives which were all built at Swindon Works between 1923 and 1951. There were 171 Castles built

Left: **Ex-GWR 3802 '2800/2884' 8F Class 2-8-0 is one of a batch of locomotives rebuilt at Swindon Works in 1938 by Collett, from a 1903 Churchward design. When this locomotive passed into BR stock (1948), its home shed was listed as Banbury (84C). Pictured in restored form, at the Llangollen Railway.**
David Gibson.

Collett on the Cambrian. Manor '78xx' Class 4-6-0 7819 'Hinton Manor'.

Collett 0-6-0PT 4602 is seen with a local stopping train at Fishguard & Goodwick Station in August 1961. *Roger Jermy.*

and the total included six engines which were rebuilt from Churchward's 'Star' Class. It is a fact that Castles were the backbone of GWR and later WR express services for over 40 years. They were as popular with the men who crewed them in the final years of BR steam as they were with the enginemen of the late 1920s.

Castles were put in charge of most of the GWR's crack express services in their heyday, and were to be seen equally at home on services to the holiday resorts of the West Country, expresses to South Wales and of course in the late 1920s and early 1930s in charge of the famous Cheltenham Flyer. The later services called for the locos to average 66.2mph, and allowed just 70 minutes to cover the 77.3 miles from Swindon to Paddington. By modern standards that may not seem a tall order but carried out on a daily basis it was an outstanding achievement of the time, for the locomotives and their footplatemen. There were many instances of 'Castle' class locomotives in charge of heavy trains topping the 100mph mark, even when in their dotage.

The first of the class 4073 'Caerphilly Castle' was displayed at the 1924 British Empire Exhibition alongside the LNER's 'Flying Scotsman'. At that time the GWR Castle 4-6-0 was the most powerful locomotive in Britain and after visiting the exhibition Nigel Gresley was reportedly 'very impressed' with the Collett locomotive. Locomotive 4073 'Caerphilly Castle' was the first of Collett's new class to enter service it did so on 23 August 1923. The four-cylinder 4-6-0 ran

5700 Class 0-6-0PT 4606 is pictured with a short freight at Westbourne Park near Paddington in 1964.

4079 'Pendennis Castle' is seen in Swindon Works being overhauled prior to preservation in February 1965. This loco went to work on a preserved railway in Australia but it is now back in the UK.

almost two million miles in service before being withdrawn in May 1960, and placed on display at the Science Museum London.

When Hawksworth became GWR CME he presided over the continuing Castle building programme. In 1948 BR became the builders of the remaining '4073' class locomotive on the order books and they built numbers 7012 to 7037 (26 engines) with 7036 'Taunton Castle' and 7037 'Swindon' being the last, both completed in August 1950. Withdrawals had started in the same year (among the six ex-'Star' rebuilds) with 4009 'Shooting Star' being the first in March 1950; the first Castle 'proper' to be scrapped was 5005 'Manorbier Castle' (built 1927) withdrawn in February 1960, with 1.7 million miles on the clock. The last in service was the 1950-built 7029 'Clun Castle' withdrawn in December 1965.

Next Collett locomotives out of 'the works' were the 56xx 0-6-2T Class in 1924 and in that same year the first of the '49xx' Hall Class 5MT 4-6-0s entered service; between 1928 and 1943 Swindon built 258 of them, which all passed into BR ownership. The numbers in use of the popular wide route availability mixed traffic type were increased between 1944 and 1950 when GWR under Hawksworth (and then BR) introduced the additional 71 locomotives of the '6959' Modified Hall 5MT 4-6-0 class.

In 1927 the GWR board's request for a more powerful locomotive to haul heavier and faster trains was complied with when Collett rolled out the first of his four-cylinder 6000 'King' Class 8P 4-6-0 locomotives. Named 'King George V' that locomotive visited the United States and to this day (in preservation) it carries a donated commemorative bell on the front buffer beam. The total number built was 30 and the last loco into service was

029, in August 1930. Initially the 22ton 10cwt axle loading of the Kings confined them to the London-Plymouth, London-Bristol and London-Wolverhampton routes. Later after permanent way improvements the class were allowed between Bristol and Shrewsbury and importantly through the Severn Tunnel into Wales.

The class were all withdrawn in 1962 the first being 6006 'King George I' in February of that year. In December the last three were taken out of service, they were 6000 'King George V', 6018 'King Henry VI' and 6025 'King Henry III'. The Kings were not necessarily taken out of service because their condition warranted it but because diesels had started to replace them on the Western Region's express trains.

In 1936 Collett's '68xx' 5MT Grange 4-6-0 class entered service and 80 were built, the last in 1939. The Grange was basically a version of the Hall class with smaller wheels. The first 20 of the Manor '78xx' Class 4-6-0s were built at the same time, with the balance following from BR in 1950. Although still rated at 5MT the Manors were a lighter version of the Grange with wider route availability, 30 were built.

Included in the large number of tank locomotives, introduced during Collett's time were 863 members of the '57xx' 3F 0-6-0PT Class. The pannier tanks were built between 1929 and 1950 not only at Swindon Works but by outside contractors Armstrong Whitworth, WG Bagnall, Beyer Peacock, Kerr Stewart, North British Locomotive Company and Yorkshire Engine Company. ∎

7812 'Erlestoke Manor' seen on the Cambrian just before it was withdrawn in 1965, note the nameplates have already been removed.

Leader of the class. 'King' Class 8P 4-6-0 6000 'King George V' is pictured hauling a very antiquated rake of stock on a special train and a GW logo on the tender, c1950. KGV visited Swindon works in early 1953 and emerged with a paint job (BR) and modifications which included remodelled outside steam pipes, cab ventilation and a stepped inside cylinder cover.

Above: **King Class 6016 'King Edward V' pictured at Laira (83D)**

Left: **5022 Wigmore Castle pictured at Wolverhampton Stafford Road (84A) in 1960.**

Right: **BR-built Collett-designed '5100' Class 4176 is seen at the head of a string of pannier tanks at Newton Abbott in 1958.**

Below: **Modified Hall 5MT 4-6-0 class 6974 'Bryngwyn Hall' and a sister loco at Newton Abbott in 1959.**

WESTERN PERFECTION

A double study in steam locomotive perfection (above) '4073' Castle Class 4-6-0 5051 'Earl Bathurst' entered service in May 1936 as 'Drysllwyn Castle' and was renamed in August 1937. This loco travelled over 1.3 million miles before being withdrawn in May 1963 and is preserved. (below) '6000' King Class 4-6-0 6000 King George V. Entered service June 1927 and travelled almost two million miles in GWR and BR service, together with others of the class it was fitted with a double chimney and blast pipe in 1955. Withdrawn in December 1962 this loco was transferred directly into preservation. The brass bell on the buffer beam and two medallions on the cabside are mementoes of 6000's visit to the USA in 1927 for the Baltimore & Ohio Railroad centenary celebrations.

THE WESTERN SCENE

The Western Region of British Railways was the January 1948 descendant of the former Great Western Railway which was itself an amalgamation of over 20 companies. Paddington Station, the former London terminus of the GWR also served the WR. The Western Region had 62 steam depots of which the principal ones were Old Oak Common (81A), Bristol Bath Road (82A), Newton Abbot (83A), Wolverhampton Stafford Road (84A), Worcester (85A), Newport Ebbw Junction (86A), Neath (87A), Cardiff Cathays (88A) and Oswestry 89A.

The Western Region initially took into stock 3856 steam locomotives from the GWR. Locomotive works acquired by the Western Region of BR were Caerphilly (opened 1899) which closed in 1963, Swindon (opened 1842) which outlasted BR steam and closed in 1986 and Wolverhampton (opened 1855) which closed in 1964.

Wolverhampton Works was credited with building 794 locomotives, the vast majority of which were tank engines. In addition to several classes of Dean 0-6-0PT engines, which lasted into BR WR tenure, the Stafford Road works also built a number of 2-6-2 Prairie Tanks to Churchward designs. The last locomotives built at Wolverhampton were 2-6-2T '4500' Class numbers 4500 to 4519 constructed between 1906 and 1908; all were taken into BR stock.

Caerphilly Works came into being in 1899 and served the Rhymney Railway passing to GWR in 1923. No locomotives were built at the works which was a repair facility only. The works, which at its peak employed 700 workers, closed in June 1963.

Swindon Works served the GWR and BR Western region right up to the end of steam and then was re-equipped in order to build diesel hydraulic locomotives. The works, which opened for business in 1842, built broad gauge locomotives for Isambard Kingdom Brunel and later converted some of those to standard gauge (and scrapped others) during the changeover in 1892/93. The highest number of employees working at the site on both locomotive construction and carriage and wagon production was recorded as being 9915.

The last GWR Chief Mechanical Engineer was Frederick William Hawksworth who served following CB Collett's retirement in 1941 until the advent of British Railways. He was a designer in his own right but in addition an 'improver'. Notably he took Collett's design for the 'Hall' class and with various modifications created the 'Modified Hall' class. Swindon Works built 71 '6959' Modified Hall Class

'1500' Class 0-6-0PT, a short wheelbase heavy shunting design with no running plate and outside cylinders, 1508 is seen at Cardiff Canton.

STEAM ERA SWINDON MILESTONES:	
April 1846	broad gauge (7ft 0 1/4in) 2-2-2 'Great Western' completed.
October 1864	last broad gauge loco built.
1896	the first 4-6-0 in England is built, locomotive number 36.
February 1908	first 4-6-2 in UK completed, 111 'The Great Bear'.
January 1, 1948	passed into BR ownership.
1950	HRH Princess Elizabeth names 'Castle' 4-6-0 7037 'Swindon'.
1955	last GWR-type locomotive built 0-6-0PT 1669.
March 1960	9F 2-10-0 92220 is rolled out. Last UK-built steam loco.

Resplendent in Great Western livery Castle Class 4-6-0 7029 'Clun Castle' is greeted by an admiring throng as 'she' heads over the river Dee towards Chester on 5 March 1967 with one of two special trains which ran to mark the end of GWR Birmingham–Birkenhead services.

Right: **Still a busy Western Region depot, Southall is pictured on a very dull June morning in 1964. Locos seen 4919 'Donnington Hall', 6944 'Fledborough Hall' and 6910 'Gossington Hall'**

Below: **Castle Class 4-6-0 5026 Criccieth Castle waits for the gates to be opened and given the road at Gabowen Station on the Shrewsbury-Chester route.**

5MT 4-6-0s which were all named and numbered 6959 to 6999 between 1944 and 1950. Locomotives numbered 6981 to 6999 were built under BR.

Hawksworth introduced his two cylinder 4-6-0 6MT '1000' Class County locomotives between 1945 and 1947. The 'Counties' were essentially a larger version of the 'Modified Hall' type. They were designed to satisfy the GWR's need for a fast mixed traffic locomotive. The class totalled 30 engines which were numbered from 1000 to 1029; all were named after English and Welsh counties. They were different in appearance from other GWR locomotives having only one long splasher over all the driving wheels with a straight nameplate mounted on the top of it. By the end of March 1965 all of the class had been scrapped.

Hawksworth also designed 4F rated pannier tanks and all were built after nationalisation. Swindon built the '1500' Class 0-6-0PT, a short wheelbase heavy shunting design with no running plate and outside cylinders. They were numbered 1500 to 1509 and after being surplus to BR requirements (1964) three of them 1501, 1502 and 1509 were sold to the National Coal Board. Locomotive number 1501 was subsequently preserved. Hawksworth's '9400' 0-6-0PT Class were built mainly by outside contractors with only 10 of the 210-strong class being Swindon products. They were the final 'pre 1948' design steam locomotives to be built; the last examples did not enter service until 1956. ∎

British Steam

The WR operated steam-hauled services from Paddington Station, London, as did its predecessor the GWR. Among the towns and cities served were Oxford, Reading, Swindon, Birkenhead via Wolverhampton, Shrewsbury and Chester, Bristol and then onwards to South Wales via the Severn Tunnel with services to Cardiff, Swansea and the ferry port of Fishguard, Hereford and the Welsh Marches, services to the West Country via Taunton, services to Torquay, Plymouth and Penzance via Yeovil and services to Gloucester, Worcester and Cheltenham Spa. The ex-GWR branch lines of the Western Region figured highly on Dr Beeching's list of closures.

The collieries and steelworks of the 'valleys' coupled with the docks of South Wales, Bristol and Avonmouth were responsible for producing a big percentage of the region's freight traffic. The china clay and mining industries of Cornwall plus oil products from the refineries of Pembrokeshire also added to the high tonnages carried. The conversion of the railways from steam to diesel power dramatically lowered the demand for Welsh coal (acclaimed by many steam loco men to have the best steaming qualities) and thus caused a huge reduction in rail freight traffic. In addition the eventual shrinkage of the steel industry lowered the number of iron ore and steel products trains to, from, and within the region. Many of Britain's redundant steam locomotives were dismantled in South Wales and the recovered metals were either converted or exported via the docks.

Above: **Ex-GWR 'Hall' Class 4-6-0 6938 'Corndean Hall' drifts through Swindon light engine, again the nameplates have been removed. 15 February 1965.**

Left: **'78xx' Manor Class 4-6-0 7824 'Ilford Manor' is pictured near the turntable at Wolverhampton Stafford Road in 1960.**

Ex-GWR Collett Mogul 2-6-0 heads past Curzon Park with a Shrewsbury-Chester train in October 1965.

Above: **Hawksworth two cylinder 4-6-0 6MT '1000' County Class 1019 'County of Merioneth' is pictured waiting to depart from Bath in 1959.**

Left: **Distinctive with one long splasher over all the driving wheels and a straight nameplate. 'County' 1004 'County of Somerset' on depot at Laira (83D) in 1961.**

Right: Seen in mint condition at Swindon is ex-GWR Mogul '43xx' Class 2-6-0 7340, the date 10 June 1961. This loco was scrapped in November 1964.

Below: '68xx' Grange Class 4-6-0 6853 'Morehampton Grange' at Tyseley (84E).

Preserved ex-Midland Railway Class 1F 0-6-0T 41708 (a type referred to as half cabs) and dating from 1880 is seen while on a visit to the Llangollen Railway. Along with five others of the class this engine saw out the end of steam at Staveley Works/Barrow Hill.

STAVELEY IRONWORKS

No BR steam enthusiast's trip to Derbyshire was complete without a visit to the Staveley Ironworks (later Stanton & Staveley) site and the adjacent engine shed and yard at Barrow Hill. The steelworks complex has long gone but fortunately the 'roundhouse' engine shed at Barrow Hill has been preserved, and it is in use as a railway heritage centre.

The important fact is that in 1866 the Midland Railway signed an agreement with the steelworks which saw it purchase the internal railway system. As part of that deal the Midland Railway was contractually obliged to supply locomotives for, and operate, the system for 100 years and that was the reason for building the Barrow Hill Roundhouse.

The building near Chesterfield is not only a unique example of 19th century railway architecture it is the last surviving operational roundhouse engine shed in the UK. It has 24 'roads' surrounding the internal turntable, the longest being 80ft and the shortest 60ft.

41763 is pictured shunting on the 'works' in 1964.

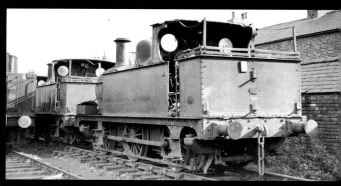

Barrow Hill/Staveley regular '1F' 0-6-0T, 41804 is seen outside the shed in September 1965. This loco was built by the Midland Railway at Derby in December 1890, rebuilt in 1915 and scrapped by BR in April 1967.

When the Midland Railway introduced its system of shed codes in 1898, Barrow Hill was given the code M24. This was later changed by the LMS to 18D in 1935. In February 1958 it changed again to 38D when the area was taken over by the Eastern region of British Railways (later changed to 41E). Steam at the depot ended on 4 October 1965 British Railways however did fulfil the 100-year agreement, which th inherited from the LMS, to supply the works with motive power

41528, another Staveley-based Deeley Midland design 0-4-0T 0F, is attracting the attention of a young enthusiast who has climbed up to have a look into the cab

WELSH HIGHLAND RAILWAY

NORTH WALES' NEWEST!

A taste of things to come: a special train for WHR 'Track Fund' Sponsor's passes through the Aberglaslyn Pass on 5th April 2008 (Original photograph by Roger Dimmick)

A Magical Mix of Steam and Scenery set in the heart of Snowdonia. Visit in 2008 and experience the thrill of the dramatic journey from Caernarfon Castle to Rhyd Ddu, high on the slopes of Snowdon...

...but don't forget to keep an eye on developments as we've nearly completed the link to the Ffestiniog Railway at Porthmadog. In fact the projected opening date is Easter 2009 - so, if you can't visit before, come ride the 'Forty Mile' railway through the Aberglaslyn Pass in 2009!

Rheilffordd Eryri / Welsh Highland Railway (Caernarfon), St Helens Road, Caernarfon, Gwynedd, LL55 2YD
enquiries@festrail.co.uk   01766 516000   www.festrail.co.uk

BLUE AND SILVER STREAMLINED
PRINCESS CORONATION PACIFIC

This is an extremely rare picture of a Stanier Princess Coronation Pacific in LMS Blue and Silver livery hauling the Coronation Scot train; only three colour images of blue and silver locomotives are thought to exist and this is one of them! The image is believed to have been taken in an early summer period of either 1938 or 1939. It is thought to be a northbound train seen under the bridge at Kingmoor, near Carlisle, where the Waverley route then crossed the West Coast Main Line.

The locomotive's identity is not known. However given that only five engines were turned out in these colours the following deductions have been made: 6220 'Coronation' is ruled out because it carried a crown symbol over the nameplate; 6221 'Queen Elizabeth' and 6224 'Princess Alexandra' carried relatively long nameplates. Therefore it has been assumed that this historically significant picture may be of either 6223 'Princess Alice' or 6222 'Queen Mary', but this may prove impossible to establish.

The image on a Dufaycolour card-mounted transparency was discovered by Gordon Hall of Hexham. It had lain forgotten and unnoticed among a collection of family photographs until discovered by accident only recently. Mr Hall has assigned the copyright of it to the National Railway Museum and we are indebted to him and the museum for allowing its reproduction. (c) National Railway Museum.

THE LOCOMOTIVE
BUILDERS
William Arthur Stanier

Although Sir William Arthur Stanier FRS (1876-1965) will long be remembered by those with a love of LMS locomotives in general, and the products of Crewe Works in particular, it should be remembered that he was a son of Wiltshire, born in the railway town of Swindon. After his formal education at Wycliffe College, Stanier joined the Great Western Railway as a 15-year-old apprentice in 1892 and studied basic GWR practices and principles in that employ until 1897. He then occupied several junior positions at Swindon until his hard work and diligence was rewarded in 1904 with a promotion to GWR Assistant Divisional Locomotive Superintendent, London.

In 1906 he moved back to Swindon to take up the position of Assistant to the Works Manager. He then became 'the' Assistant Works Manager in 1912 and in 1920 was appointed to the post of Swindon Works Manager. In 1922 he gained a further promotion to Principal Assistant to the Chief Mechanical Engineer of the GWR Mr CB Collett. In the world of locomotive engineering the talents of Stanier had been noticed, and he was destined for greater things.

But not with the GWR for the directors had made it plain that they wanted Collett to stay in post until he was 70 years old and that would have made Stanier 65! At the GWR Stanier lived in the shadow of Collett, a situation he accepted for 10 years. It was a period of intense learning and when he left the GWR for pastures new in 1932 he took with him all of the experience gained from working in Collett's team. He also took with him a chest containing invaluable steam locomotive engineering drawings which he had collected during his working life; they represented over 40 years of Swindon knowledge.

So fully equipped for the challenge William Arthur Stanier joined the LMS in 1932 as their CME and that marked the beginning of what many refer to as the 'Golden Age' of steam locomotive building at Crewe. However it was not all plain sailing and Stanier's first task was to mould the somewhat disjointed management teams (at the various LMS works) into one cohesive and progressive unit. He succeeded in doing just that. The total number of ex- LMSR steam locomotives taken into stock by British Railways was 7805 of which some 2430 were attributable to Stanier.

In June 1933 the first of Stanier's Pacifics emerged from Crewe works in the shape of 4-6-2 No 6200 'The Princess Royal'. These fine four-cylinder locomotives gave exemplary service to both the LMS and the London Midland Region of BR for over 27 years on express passenger trains. As diesels started to be introduced during the 1950s some of the class were put into store. They were taken back into service to cover busy summer timetables but withdrawal of the whole class was imminent, it took place between October 1961 and November 1962. In 1936 6201(LMS number) 'Princess Elizabeth' set a steam record hauling a seven-coach train between London Euston and Glasgow covering the 401 miles in five hours, 53 minutes and 38 seconds.

There were 13 of the class built and two examples 46201 'Princess Elizabeth' and 46203 'Princess Margaret Rose' were preserved. One member of the class (4)6202 was constructed as a turbine-driven steam locomotive (nicknamed Turbomotive) and ran in that form until 1950 when it was converted back to a conventional locomotive. Unfortunately 46202 was wrecked and judged to be beyond economical repair in the Harrow and Wealdstone disaster of October 1952.

Just prior to the introduction of the Princess Royal class, Stanier's successful 5MT 2-6-0 'Moguls' were introduced, a Crewe build totalling 40 engines. Like the 'Princess Royals' they too featured boilers used for the first time by the LMS, which became known as 'Stanier tapered boilers'. The first Stanier 'Black Five' 5MT 4-6-0s were taken into service during 1934 and this prolific class in various guises was continually built by the LMS, two subcontractors and BR for the best part of 17 years.

The Crewe Works model of Blue and Silver Princess Coronation 4-6-2 8P 6221 'Queen Elizabeth'

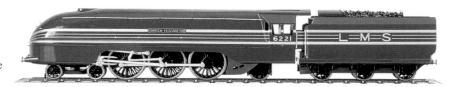

June 1937 saw the exciting introduction of Mr Stanier's Princess Coronation 8P Class of 4-6-2 Pacifics, the first 10 of which, and a later batch of 14, were streamlined. Hauled by 'Princess Coronation' locomotives the streamlined Coronation Scot train was introduced as a 'total concept' in order to achieve fast travel between London Euston and Glasgow Central. The specially designed carriage sets were built at the LMS carriage works Wolverton.

The first five of these engines, numbered 6220-6224, were streamlined with what was described by many observers at the time as a 'bathtub' shroud shape of steel air smoothed casing. They were painted in a distinctive blue and silver chevron-striped livery. A further five streamlined locomotives were outshopped from Crewe in the following year, numbered 6225-6229, and they were also adorned with the chevron stripes, however, they were

finished in a maroon and gilt colour scheme. The LMS publicity stated that they, too, would work Scottish expresses but additionally London-Liverpool trains.

The remaining members of the class were delivered to the LMS between 1939 and 1943, and locomotives 6230-6234 were built without air smooth casing; however, the next batch, numbered 6235-6248, were built as streamliners. A further batch of seven locos (6249-6255) was built without streamlining. The last two (46256 and 46257) were also unstreamlined but built after Stanier's reign, by his successor HG Ivatt, who made modifications that included the fitting of roller bearings and a redesigned trailing truck.

During 1945-1949 the streamlining was removed from all of the class, after which they appeared in five different liveries, lined black, lined green, two shades of blue and lined maroon. The last engine to lose its streamlining was

Above: **Stanier 8F 2-8-0 48119 is seen drifting slowly through the Cheshire countryside towards Northwich. This 8F was built at Crewe in 1939, withdrawn in November 1967 (only three months after this picture was taken) and cut up in April 1968.**

Left: **Crewe 1934-built Stanier 2-6-0 5MT 42958 seen on shed at Willesden (1A) in 1964, this loco was scrapped in June 1966.**

Below: **North British-built Jubilee Class 45563 Australia is seen leaving Chester with a train of vans for Holyhead. The yellow stripe on the cab side indicates that the loco could not work south of Crewe 'under the wires', August 1965.**

46243 'City of Lancaster' in September 1949. These powerful locomotives became the main choice motive power for the LMS Anglo Scottish express trains of the post WWII era. Withdrawals started to take place in 1962 and all 38 of the class had disappeared from BR metals by 1964. Three locomotives from the class numbers 46229, 46233 and 46235 were preserved.

In all, Stanier introduced to the LMS 11 classes of engine between 1933 and 1943, including the Jubilee 4-6-0; 2-6-2 and 2-6-4 tank locomotives; and the very successful 8F 2-8-0 freight locomotives. He instigated the conversion of 70 Royal Scot 4-6-0s in 1943, which were originally a 1927 Fowler design for the LMS. He retired as CME to the LMS in 1944, having been knighted for his services to the railway industry a year earlier. Sir William Stanier FRS died in September 1965, at Rickmansworth, Hertfordshire. ■

Above: **The easily identified slope on the smokebox front shows that Princess Coronation 4-6-2 46246 'City of Manchester' was once streamlined (casing removed 1946). That feature caused the young enthusiasts of the day to dub such engines 'Semis' (ie semi-streamlined). 46246 is pictured with Princess Class Royal 46203 'Princess Margaret Rose' at Glasgow Polmadie in April 1956.** *David Anderson*

Left: **Stanier Jubilee 4-6-0 is true to its name. Seen nearing the summit of Beattock with a Liverpool/Manchester-Glasgow train in 1958. The loco is number 45731, its name 'Perseverance'.** *David Anderson*

An atmospheric Crewe scene from 1956. Princess Coronations meet while the permanent way gang look on. 46220 'Coronation' and 46222 'Queen Mary'. *Peter Kerslake*

THE **LONDON** **MIDLAND SCENE**

The London Midland Region of British Railways, which came into being in January 1948, was effectively the post-grouping London Midland & Scottish Railway. The LMSR created in 1923 was an amalgamation of 14 principal companies, many locomotives of which were taken into BR stock. Of the four companies making up BR the ex-LMSR supplied 7805, by far the biggest number of steam locomotives.

Stanier 5MT 4-6-0 climbing Gresford Bank in 1967. This was a Vulcan Foundry-built example of the class.

Stanier 5MT 4-6-0 (Black Five) 45426 is pictured near Warrington in 1960. This Armstrong Whitworth-built engine was cut up in August 1968.

The principal route of the LMR was the West Coast Main Line which connected London, Birmingham, Liverpool and Manchester with Scotland. When newly created the LMR had 140 operational motive power depots.

The main district depots were: Willesden (1A), Rugby (2A), Bescot (3A), Bletchley (4A), Crewe North (5A), Chester (6A), Llandudno Junction (7A), Edge Hill (8A), Longsight (9A), Springs Branch (10A), Carnforth (11A), Carlisle Upperby (12A), Cricklewood (14A), Wellingborough (15A), Nottingham (16A), Derby (17A), Toton (18A), Sheffield (19A), Leeds (20A), Saltley (21A), Bristol (22A), Skipton (23A), Accrington (24A), Wakefield (25A), Newton Heath (26A), Bank Hall (27A) and Blackpool (28A).

Stanier 8F 48542 is pictured approaching High Bentham from Low Bentham in August 1965.

A total of six locomotive works from the region passed into BR ownership, they were: Bow (opened 1850) which closed in 1960; Crewe dating from 1843 which remained open throughout the whole existence of British Railways (and beyond in private ownership); Derby which opened in 1840 and also outlasted BR; Horwich (opened 1887) which closed as steam was discontinued in 1968; Kilmarnock (opened 1856) which closed in 1959 and St Rollox (Glasgow) which also outlasted the steam era.

Bow Locomotive Works was opened by the North London Railway and built its last locomotive in 1906 before coming under LNWR control two years later. The site became a repair-only centre and survived nationalisation but was closed 12 years later with its work being taken over by Derby. Crewe Works, which had built the majority of the LMS stock transferred in 1948, supplied steam locomotives to BR until December 1958 when its 7331st steam locomotive was rolled out.

Derby Works completed its first steam locomotives in 1831. The famous first main line diesel Co-Co number 10000 was built there in 1947. The last LMSR

locomotive to be built there, Class 2 2-6-2T 41329, left the works in June 1952. BR Standard-type steam locomotives were built at Derby between 1951 and 1957. The centre served BR up to the end of steam as a repair facility but by that time was also heavily involved in diesel work.

Horwich Works was built to serve the Lancashire & Yorkshire Railway. The site passed into LNWR ownership in 1922, became part of LMSR in 1923 and BR LMR at the time of nationalisation. The works produced a great many of the steam locomotives which passed into BR ownership. Between 1887 and 1948 Horwich produced 1668 steam locomotives and thereafter a further 162 including BR Standard types. In 1958 the works produced the first BR diesel-electric shunting locomotive, the last locomotive built there was D4157, an 0-6-0 diesel-electric shunter, outshopped in 1962.

The first steam locomotive was built at Kilmarnock Locomotive Works in 1857 and the last (the 392nd) in 1921. Under British Railways Kilmarnock Works operated as a repair facility which from 1952 also included the maintenance of railway cranes. St Rollox (Glasgow) was opened by the Caledonian Railway, becoming part of the LMSR in 1923. The first locomotive was built there in 1854 and the last 4476, an 0-6-0 type, in 1928. Thereafter the workshops became a locomotive and carriage repair centre. In 1962 St Rollox/Glasgow Works was extensively reorganised in order to become the main BR works in Scotland. The site continued to fulfil that role after the steam era.

In addition to Sir William A Stanier several other renowned locomotive builders (CMEs) of the 20th century are represented by the ex-LMSR steam stock

STEAM ERA CREWE MILESTONES:

1845	locomotive number 49 'Columbine' completed.
1866	1000th locomotive built, DX Class 0-6-0 No 613.
1911	5000th locomotive built, 4-4-0 No 5000 'Coronation'.
1937	First streamlined Princess Coronation built, 6220 'Coronation'.
1950	7000th locomotive built, Ivatt 2-6-2T No 41272.
1951	First BR Standard Class locomotive built, 4-6-2 70000 'Britannia'.
1958	Last steam locomotive built, 2-10-0 9F No 92250
1967	Last steam locomotive repaired, 4-6-2 70013 'Oliver Cromwell'.

Jubilee Class 4-6-0 5596 'Bahamas' (LMS number) is pictured in LMS red soon after being saved for preservation. It is seen at Dinting in November 1969.

Princess Coronation 4-6-2 46240 'City of Coventry' is pictured just about to move off shed at Willesden. Built by the LMS in 1940 the loco was withdrawn in October 1964 and cut up two months later.

A 1925 post-grouping Caledonian design. This 2P 0-4-4T locomotive was one of 10 which went into first LMS and then BR service. 55261 is seen shunting coaching stock at Carstairs Junction in 1956. Note the express passenger headlamp code! This loco survived in BR service until September 1961. *David Anderson*

This 3/4 front view helps to explain why the Hughes/Fowler 5MT 2-6-0s earned the nickname 'Crabs'. Horwich-built 42708 is seen at Castleton in 1962. This engine was withdrawn in July 1964.

This Patriot Class 4-6-0, 45517 was one of several that were never given names. The unrebuilt Fowler 6P5F is seen with a Glasgow-Blackpool excursion on the WCML at Crawford in 1960. This loco was Crewe built in 1933. *David Anderson*

inherited by the London Midland Region. They include: George Hughes (formerly L&Y) 1932-1925, Sir Henry Fowler 1925-1931 (formerly MR), Charles E Fairburn 1944-1945 and Henry George Ivatt 1945-1947 from the LMS, William Pickersgill (1914-1923) from the Caledonian Railway and Charles John Bowen-Cooke (1909-1920) from the LNWR.

The main terminus of the LMR was London's famous Euston Station serving the WCML. Glasgow Central was the main Scottish station arrived at via Rugby Midland, Crewe, Preston (for Blackpool) and Carlisle, with additional services to Edinburgh via Carstairs. Euston also served Coventry, Birmingham and the Midlands. St Pancras connected with services to Bedford, Leicester, Nottingham and Sheffield and an alternative route to Manchester. Marylebone also served the capital with other services to the Midlands and the North via Aylesbury and Rugby Central.

Crewe on the WCML was central to the operation of the region with not just the 'works' but two motive power depots and routes to Derby, Nottingham and the East Midlands via Stafford, a direct line to Shrewsbury, the main line to Holyhead via Chester, a connection with Manchester Piccadilly via Stockport and a through route to Liverpool via Weaver Junction. There were extensive services on the cross-Pennine routes between Liverpool, Manchester and various Yorkshire destinations including Bradford via Rochdale and Leeds via Huddersfield. The electrified Woodhead route also came under control of the region. The scenic Settle & Carlisle route and the long lamented Somerset & Dorset also became part of the LMR. With myriad interconnecting and secondary routes the LMR was a very complex network, which before Beeching had a large number of duplicate routes and branch lines.

All three London LMR terminals handled high volumes of commuter trains, the majority being steam hauled. Freight traffic was heavy on all routes with coal trains perhaps being the most prolific. The region's railways also served several steel-producing areas, the quarries of Cumbria, Derbyshire and Wales, the chemical works of the North West and the car builders and 'metal bashers' of the West Midlands. Petroleum products, specifically from the Stanlow Refinery near Ellesmere Port, and trains serving the various docks in the region also added to the high volume of freight.

Fresh produce was also carried by the railways, for example express 'fish trains' were a regular sight on the WCML taking Aberdeen and Fleetwood-landed catches to the wholesale markets of the UK. Livestock trains were often a feature of the services to the port of Holyhead and to and from Scotland. 'Soap Flake City' (a local railway name for Warrington) produced a large number of van trains conveying products guaranteed to get your whites whiter! ■

Above: **A pre-BR scene at Heaton Mersey MPD (9F) in 1946.**

Right: **Standing in 1961 at what since 2008 has been a St Pancras Eurostar platform is Royal Scot Class 4-6-0 46112 'Sherwood Forester'. Built by North British Locomotive Company in 1927 and then rebuilt by the LMS in 1947.**

Above: **Johnson Midland 'Jinty' 0-6-0T was built by Vulcan Foundry in 1901 and withdrawn from BR service in 1964. It is pictured at Walton depot (27E) and is fitted with condensing gear.**

Left: **43361 an 0-6-0 loco of Midland 3F design dating from 1885 and pictured at Kilnhurst c1957.**

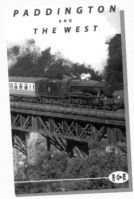

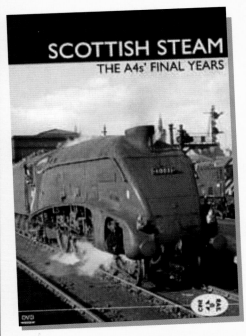

THE LOCOMOTIVE
BUILDERS
Herbert Nigel Gresley

Herbert Nigel Gresley (1876-1941) was born in Edinburgh and educated at Marlborough School. Gresley is considered by many to be 'The King' of locomotive builders which is appropriate as he started his railway career at Crewe Works in 1897 as an apprentice under another railway hero Francis William Webb who was the undisputed 'King of Crewe'. Gresley was a diligent pupil and by all accounts a quick learner, after five years of schooling he moved into the works at LNWR before joining the burgeoning Lancashire & Yorkshire Railway in 1898.

I n 1901 he was promoted to the post of Assistant Works Manager at Newton Heath Carriage & Wagon Works and again in 1902 to Works Manager. He joined the Great Northern Railway in 1905 as C&W Superintendent and in 1911 became the GNR Locomotive Engineer. He held that position until the time of 'Grouping' in 1923 when he was appointed Chief Mechanical Engineer to the London North Eastern Railway. He was awarded the CBE in 1920 and was knighted in 1936. Sir Herbert Nigel Gresley CBE died 'in service', after a short illness on 5 April 1941.

In 1948 British Railways took into stock 6525 steam locomotives from the LNER; Gresley was associated with the original design (or rebuilding) of some 1739 of those. In all Gresley introduced or improved 26 different types of steam locomotives varying from 0-6-0Ts to his much-acclaimed A4 Pacifics which in streamlined form served both the LNER and then BR from 1935 until the early 1960s. The first A4 (which was a development of the successful A3 design) 60014 'Silver Link' emerged from Doncaster Works to great acclaim in 1935, the three-cylinder 4-6-2s were a sensation right from the start. The travelling public loved them.

The first four built 2509-2512 (LNER numbers) were given a silver livery and hauled the 'Silver Jubilee' train between London and Newcastle, which they did in less than four hours. The A4s were all built at Doncaster Locomotive Works. In 1951 BR gave the class an 8P power rating. The early build A4s had valances over the driving wheels but they were permanently removed after only a short time, to facilitate maintenance. The engines proved themselves in service on the fast heavy express trains of the East Coast Main Line, regularly running at speeds around 100mph.

Left: **Pictured after the end of steam on BR, Gresley 'A3' Pacific 4472 'Flying Scotsman' (BR number 60103) is seen on the WCML at Shap with two tenders attached during a special run in July 1969. The locomotive never ran in LNER or BR service with two tenders but made several runs in preservation with them. The second tender allowed 11,000 gallons of water to be carried thus increasing the loco's range between service stops. The main tender carried the letters LNER and the second one carried the number 4472.**

Gresley 'V3' Class 2-6-2, 67624 is pictured with a local stopping train on the Edinburgh Suburban Line.
David Anderson.

Ex-LNER Gresley 'D49' Class 4-4-0 62718 'Kinross-shire' is pictured heading south having just crossed the Forth Bridge.
David Anderson.

The East Coast Main Line at Dalmeny station in 1955. Gresley 'V2' Class 2-6-2 6MT 60824 is seen departing with an Aberdeen/Dundee-Edinburgh Waverley Service. This loco was withdrawn in November 1966.
David Anderson.

Preparing to leave the shed. Gresley 'A3' 4-6-2 60036 'Windsor Lad' pictured at Haymarket (64B). Built in 1927 this locomotive was withdrawn by BR in 1961.
David Anderson.

'A4' 60024 'Kingfisher' is pictured being coaled at the Nine Elms depot in March 1966 after working a Waterloo-Exeter special.

Most of the class of 35 engines were given corridor tenders, thus allowing crew changes during the long non-stop runs. The railway world really sat up and took notice when on 7 July 1938 A4 4468 'Mallard' (BR number 60022) broke the world speed record for steam locomotives, that speed of 126.5 mph has never been bettered. There was a slight down side to the run however while breaking the record 'Mallard' melted all the 'bearing metal' in her middle big-end, the loco was towed back to her home shed!

No account of Gresley's achievements, however brief, would be complete without reference to the iconic locomotive 4472 'Flying Scotsman' (BR number 60103); the 4-6-2 'A3' is one of the most famous steam locomotives in the world. It is one of a class of 79 'A1/A3/A10' Class 7P6F 4-6-2s built/rebuilt at Doncaster Works (engines 60035-60063 and 60084-60112) and North British Locomotive Company Glasgow (engines 60064-60083). Engine 60068 came into BR stock as an A10 and was converted to A3 in 1948. From 1928 a total of 26 engines were built new as A3 types while the rest were originally A1s and then A10s, subsequently rebuilt as A3s between 1927 and 28. They were fast runners with several of the class including 'Flying Scotsman' topping 100mph and over. The class served the LNER and then BR well, most remaining in service until the early 1960s.

It would be wrong to portray Gresley as only being a builder of express locomotives; he was also responsible for a varied selection of types including some highly successful freight engines. There are 16 steam locomotive types with which he was associated during his reign at the LNER. That number included in 1926 'J38' O-6-0 and 'J39' 0-6-0, in 1927 'D49' 4-4-0, in 1928 'A3' 4-6-2 and 'B17' 4-6-0, in 1930 'V1' 2-6-2T, in 1935 'A4' 4-6-2, and in 1936 'V2' 2-6-2T. History has judged Gresley as a truly great locomotive builder but due to the ruling LNER policies at the time his built totals are low (compared with CMEs of other companies) tempting the remark 'it's quality not quantity that counts!' ■

Right: **Gresley A4 Pacific 60012 'Commonwealth of Australia' passing Haymarket with a 10am Edinburgh Waverley-Glasgow Queen Street service.**
David Anderson.

Below: **Gresley Masterpiece. World steam speed record holder 60022 'Mallard' (126.5 mph) is pictured at King's Cross on 2 June 1962, waiting to depart with the London King's Cross-York-Selby-Newcastle-Edinburgh Waverley leg of the RCTS/SLS Aberdeen Flyer Railtour. This locomotive is part of the National Collection.**
David Anderson.

Liverpool Street Station in November 1960, note the parcels awaiting loading. The loco is 69614, a 1923 Stratford-built LNER 'N7 Class' 0-6-2T. It is an original N7 rebuilt with a round top Gresley boiler and thus was reclassified as N7/4.

THE **EASTERN SCENE**

The Eastern Region of British Railways (post-1948) was a section of the post-grouping London North Eastern Railway (LNER). In 1922 the LNER was formed by the amalgamation of nine railway companies of which the principal members were the Great Northern Railway, the North Eastern Railway, the Great Eastern Railway, the Great Central Railway and the North British Railway.

Darlington-built Gresley Sandringham 'Class B17 'Houghton Hall' is seen at Liverpool Street Station in 1957. This locomotive served BR until September 1959.

The Eastern Region served London, part of Yorkshire (generally south of Doncaster), Lincolnshire and East Anglia and parts of Leicestershire, but its territory also included Gorton, Greater Manchester, Peterborough ex-London Midland and Staveley. Interestingly locomotives carrying ex-LNER numbers (ie in the series 60000 to 69999) were often to be found on what could be described as foreign (or shared) territory. Listed are just a few examples: Trafford Park (9E), Northwich (9G later 8E), Wrexham (6E), Cricklewood (14A), Bidston (6F) and Brunswick (8E) were among the LMR steam depots which post-1948 retained ex-LNER locomotive allocations.

There were 50 steam motive power depots in the ER of which the principal ones were Stratford (30A), Cambridge (31A), Norwich (32A), Plaistow (33A), King's Cross (34A), New England (35A), Doncaster (36A), Ardsley (37A), Colwick (38A), Gorton (39A) and Lincoln (40A). There were three depots in Yarmouth, they were South Town (32D), Vauxhall (32E) and Beach (32F).

King's Cross is famously the London terminus of the East Coast Main Line where traditionally LNER express services serving the north of England and Scotland emanated from. Liverpool Street Station dealt with services between the capital and East Anglia while both stations handled a high degree of commuter traffic. The former Great Central Railways prestigious London terminal was Marylebone and it became part of the Eastern Region of the BR, but after 10 years passed into BR Midland Region administration. On Sunday 4 September 1966 the final train (a Marylebone to Nottingham BR MR service) ran over what remained of the Great Central Railway, and it then ceased to be a trunk route.

The region carried big volumes of freight from the industrial North East, plus heavy coal trains from Nottinghamshire and Yorkshire, and steel from the Scunthorpe area. The ports of Tilbury, Harwich, Felixstowe, Yarmouth and Boston generated varying levels of freight traffic. Bananas were imported at Boston and together with fresh produce from the area were shipped south. The sugar beet industry of Lincolnshire also generated freight traffic and fish trains regularly left the, then thriving, fishing port of Grimsby destined for markets in all parts of the country.

Three of the six ex-LNER locomotive works acquired by British Railways were in BR Eastern Region territory. Stratford Works was opened by the Great Eastern Railway Company in 1847 and turned out its first steam locomotives some three years later. The works became part of the LNER in 1923 and built its last steam locomotive in 1924, an N7 Class 0-6-2T; over 1700 steam locomotives were built at Stratford. The works became part of BR in 1948 and in the 1950s was re-equipped in order to repair diesel-electric locomotives. The works closed in 1962 but the MPD continued to be used throughout the BR steam era.

Gorton Locomotive Works, Manchester was known locally as 'The Tank'. It was opened to serve the Manchester, Sheffield & Lincolnshire Railway Company in 1848 and became part of the LNER in 1923. Its last, and 1006th steam locomotive, was built under British Railways in 1949, it was a B1 'Class' 4-6-0 number 61349. Thereafter Gorton built 64 locomotives of the 1500 v dc electric type, outshopping the last in 1954. The works closed in 1962, at the time of the BR workshops reorganisation programme.

The busiest of the region's works was Doncaster which is not only famous in its own right but for its association with Sir Nigel Gresley, 'Mallard' and of course 'Flying Scotsman'. The extensive workshops were completed in 1853 for the Great Northern Railway. Under the LNER Doncaster produced not only steam but diesel and electric locomotives, it became part of BR ER on 1 January 1948.

The last LNER-designed steam loco built at the works was A1 'Class' 4-6-2 number 60162, completed in December 1949. Doncaster's first BR Standard emerged from the workshops in December 1952 and the last steam locomotive built there was another BR Standard a Class 4' 2-6-0 number 76114, completed in October 1957. In total 2223 steam locomotives were built at Doncaster over a period of 104 years. What remains of the works is today in private ownership, and still serves the UK's railway industry. ■

Robinson-designed 'Large Director' D11 4-4-0 62660 'Butler-Henderson' built at Gorton in 1949, is preserved as part of the national collection. It is pictured in action during 1987 at the Great Central Railway. In 2008 it was a static exhibit at the National Railway Museum.

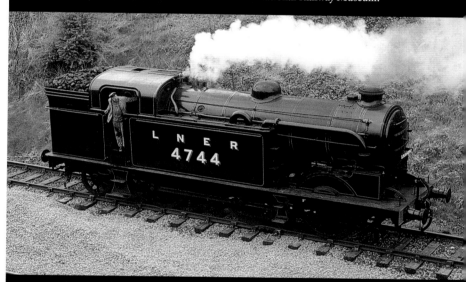

Preserved Gresley N2 0-6-2T was allocated to King's Cross on delivery from North British Locomotive Company Glasgow in 1921 and remained there until withdrawn in May 1962. It is pictured as restored in 1978.

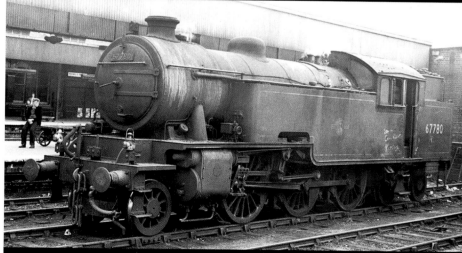

The LNER Thompson-designed 'L1 Class' 2-6-4T types were originally built to work suburban services out of King's Cross and Marylebone. Locomotive 67780 was built in 1950 by Robert Stephenson & Hawthorn, the 4MT L1s were the most powerful 2-6-4Ts to run on BR. This example is seen 'between turns' at Doncaster in June 1961, it was cut up in March 1963.

You can almost hear the beat of the engines in this evocative picture.
Two of Sir Nigel Gresley's finest creations head from Haymarket Shed
to Edinburgh Waverley Station to link up with their rostered trains.
When footplate crews spotted photographers at this location they
inevitably put on a show and this occasion was no exception!
Class A3 7P 4-6-2 60083 'Sir Hugo' leads A4 8P Pacific 60011
'Empire of India'. *David Anderson.*

Ex-NER P3 0-6-0 is seen in restored form during a 1992 visit to the Llangollen Railway. This locomotive was built at Darlington in 1923 for the North Eastern Railway. Under the LNER the P3s were reclassified as J27s, under the LNER renumbering scheme No 2392 became No 5894. Under BR it then became 65894 and carried that identification until the end of its BR career, in September 1967.

THE NORTH EASTERN SCENE

The North Eastern Region of British Railways (post-1948) was the remaining section of the post-grouping London North Eastern Railway. The NER of BR served a large area of Yorkshire and the whole of the North East of England. There were 32 steam depots in the region and the principal ones were York (50A), Darlington (51A), Gateshead (52A), Hull (53A), and Sunderland (54A). York (now the home of the National Railway Museum) was an important railway centre on the Anglo Scottish route via the East Coast Main Line. Hull boasted three locomotive depots Dairycoates (53A), Botanic Gardens (53B) and Springhead (53C).

A line-up of three Wordsell 'J26' 0-6-0s seen at Thornaby (51L) in 1960. From this class of 50 engines, 30 were built at Darlington and 20 (including 65777) at Gateshead.

York, the starting point for the line to Scarborough and then Whitby, is also linked by main lines to Leeds, Selby and Hull, and to other parts of the region by secondary routes. In addition to the port of Hull and the region of Humberside the docks at Goole and Immingham were also served by the NER. To the north the NER linked Middlesbrough, Sunderland, Newcastle and all the industrial centres of Teeside and Tyneside with the rest of the UK rail network.

The NER joined with two cross-country routes to the 'west and Carlisle', one via the railway centre of Darlington and thence Kirby Stephen, and the other via Hexham, Haltwhistle and Brampton Junction. Not forgetting that the area is considered to be the birthplace of 'the railway' by virtue of the celebrated Stockton and Darlington Railway, which officially opened on 27 September 1825.

ex-LNER 4-6-2 'A1' Pacific 60129 is seen under the impressive roof of Darlington Station in 1960.

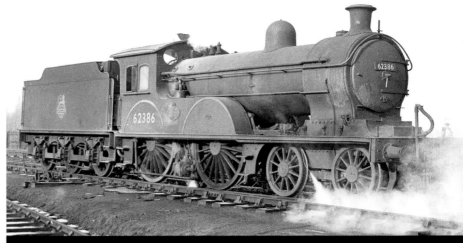

D20 4-4-0 number 62386, a Wilson Wordsell design for the NER. This loco was built at Gateshead Works in September 1907 and was scrapped when 50 years old in 1957.

The railway works at Darlington was inherited by BR in 1948; it was originally built by the S&DR (1863) became part of the NER and later the LNER, in 1923. Darlington Works continued to build steam locomotives until 1957 and in 94 years of operation produced 2269 engines. The first locomotive built was an 0-6-0 type in 1864, it was numbered 175 and named 'Contractor'. The last steam loco was a BR Standard 'Class 2' 2-6-2T number 84029, which was outshopped in June 1957. The last Darlington-built locomotive was a 'Class 25' Bo-Bo diesel electric number D7597, completed in 1964. BR closed the works on 2 April 1966.

Another works which contributed to the ex-LNER pool of steam locomotives was Gateshead Works which had an association with the Newcastle & Darlington Junction Railway (1844). The works passed into NER and then LNER ownership and was closed in 1932. It gains a mention here, under BR NER, because it was reopened in 1939 as a repair shop fulfilling that role until being finally closed by BR in 1959. ∎

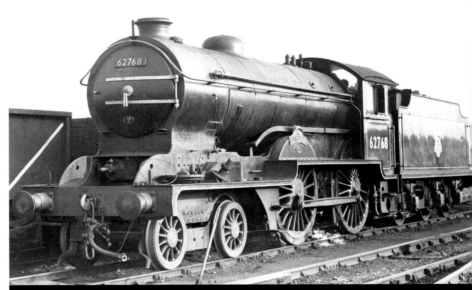

LNER Darlington-built Gresley (three-cylinder as introduced) D49 'Hunt Class' 4-4-0 62768 'The Morpeth is pictured at York in 1951. This loco was prematurely withdrawn in October 1952 after suffering collision damage. Built in 1934 it was rebuilt by Thompson in 1942 with two inside cylinders, in a configuration which had its origins in the D11 Director class, it was then reclassified as D49/4.

Darlington-built 'Class L1' Thompson-designed 2-6-4T 7715 is seen outside the works in 1960.

Another Gateshead-built loco this time dating from 1900. D20 4-4-0 number 62360 is pictured in the 1950s at Northallerton Station.

Crewe-built Stanier 6P5F Jubilee 4-6-0 45702 'Colossus' seen in full cry at Elvanfoot with an evening express from Glasgow Central to Liverpool/Manchester.
David Anderson.

JUBILEES AT WORK ON THE WCML

The 'Jubilee Class' was introduced between 1934 and 1936, LMS number series 5552–5742, British Railways 45552–45742, all were named. They entered service at the same time as the 'Black Fives' but unlike that class the Jubilees were not immediately successful as they were poor steamers. Following the rectification of those problems the class became good performers and handled varied express passenger duties with great success, particularly on former Midland Railway routes. Two members of the class (45735/36) were rebuilt in 1942 with larger boilers, double chimneys and smoke deflectors making them virtually indistinguishable from the rebuilt 'Royal Scot' class. Four examples are preserved.

BUILD DETAILS

Crewe Works 131, North British Locomotive Co Ltd 50, Derby Works 10, total built 191.

A Crewe built Jubilee 6P5F 4-6-0 on freight duty. 45716 'Swiftsure' heads south from Elvanfoot.
David Anderson.

70013 'OLIVER CROMWELL' AT WORK ON THE WCML

BR Standard 4-6-2 7P6F 70013 'Oliver Cromwell' was outshopped from Crewe Works in May 1951 and worked to the end of steam on BR. The loco was one of four which between them hauled the famous goodbye to steam 'Fifteen Guinea Special' on 11 August 1968. The preserved Standard Pacific is pictured near Warrington in April 1968 with a railtour and (below) at Moore in charge of a 'down' parcels on a misty 4 November 1967.

THE LOCOMOTIVE
BUILDERS
Henry George Ivatt

Due to his strong family ties it is hard to imagine Henry George Ivatt following any other profession than locomotive engineer. His father was the great locomotive builder Henry Alfred Ivatt, Chief Engineer of the North Eastern Railway from 1896 to 1911, and his brother-in-law was Southern Region (and for a short while BR SR) CME Oliver Vaughan Snell Bulleid. Surely the 'gentlemen's' after-dinner conversations at Ivatt family gatherings must have centred around only one subject!

When 'Ivatt the younger' was an LNWR Crewe Works apprentice he was a colleague of one Robert Arthur Riddles, and their careers became closely linked. Prior to the onset of WWI Ivatt had risen through the ranks to the post of Assistant Outdoor Machinery Superintendent at Crewe while Riddles was employed as a fitter at Rugby. After the war Ivatt had a spell with the North Staffordshire Railway at Stoke-on-Trent while Riddles returned to Rugby for a time before becoming Assistant to the Works Manager at Crewe; we shall return to his story later.

Ivatt became Special Assistant to Henry Fowler at Derby Works and in 1928 was promoted to the post of Works Superintendent. During the famous 'Stanier era' Ivatt became Mechanical Engineer Scotland (LMS) but as war loomed again in 1939 he was seconded to war preparation work, which included overseeing the building of 5000 'Tanks' (the fighting variety).

After the cessation of hostilities Ivatt resumed railway work at the LMS as Principal Assistant to Stanier.

'HG' continued in that role after Stanier's resignation in 1944, serving his successor Charles Edward Fairburn. Fairburn's reign as CME was cut short by his premature death in 1945. As a consequence in January 1946 Ivatt became Chief Mechanical Engineer of the LMS. He continued in that role through the birth of British Railways (1948) becoming CME of that organisation until his retirement in June 1951. Under the LMS, and later BR, he was responsible for the production of 420 'new era' steam locomotives, which were the forerunners of the BR Standard types.

There were three new types produced under Ivatt's tenure although it is fair to say that two of them were in fact 'twins', a Class 2MT tender type and a Class 2MT tank locomotive, which had identical principal dimensions and power ratings. The LMS, in common

Above: **Ivatt 2-6-0 4MT 43138 is pictured in full cry with a heavy coal train traversing the Edinburgh South Side Suburban Line; if you listen carefully you can hear the bark of the exhaust!** *David Anderson.*

with other railways, needed a small easy-to-maintain modern locomotive to replace its near life-expired and 'war weary' fleet of '2' power class engines. For the tender version Ivatt preferred the 2-6-0 'Mogul' wheel arrangement, he added a trailing wheel (to support the coal tender weight) making the 'tank' version a 2-6-2T.

The first locomotives of both configurations went into production at Crewe Works, and early batches of both were made available for LMS service in December 1946.

The Ivatt Class 2s were ideal for branch line and other light work and their cab arrangement gave footplate crews a real degree of comfort and protection from the elements with side window cabs as standard. Both types incorporated cut-away tender sides to improve vision when running tender first. They were easier to maintain than the locomotives which they replaced and in addition were fitted with rocking grates, self-cleaning smokeboxes and self-emptying ashpans.

BUILD DETAILS IVATT 2-6-0 CLASS 2MT, 128 LOCOMOTIVES BUILT

Crewe	46400-46464	1946 to 1950
Darlington	46465-46502	1951 to 1952
Swindon	46503-46527	1952 to 1952

Seven examples survived into preservation. The Swindon-built locomotives included BR Standard features, common to the 'Class 2' 2-6-0, 78000 types.

BUILD DETAILS IVATT 2-6-2T CLASS 2MT, 130 LOCOMOTIVES BUILT

Crewe	41200-41319	1946 to 1952
Derby	41320-41329	1952

Above: **Crew change on 46411 at Manchester Victoria c1960.**

Left: **Preserved Crewe-built Ivatt Mogul 2-6-0 2MT 46441 is pictured back at the famous works on the occasion of the Great Gathering in September 2005.**

Right: **The 'first' of the class. Ivatt Mogul 4MT 43000 is pictured over the ash pit at Carlisle Upperby (12A) in 1963. This loco was withdrawn in September 1967.**

Below: **Ivatt 'Class 2MT' 2-6-2T 41318 is pictured working 'tender first' at Exeter Central in 1958.**

Unsurprisingly both types were well received by locomotive crews and running shed staff in all regions. After some early 'draughting' problems were overcome (following experiments at Swindon and Derby) they became solid and reliable performers. The first 'Class 2' 2-6-0s were withdrawn in 1962 and the last in 1967. The first of both classes to be withdrawn was in 1962 and the last in 1967.

Locomotive No 41272 had the distinction of being the 7000th steam engine to be built at Crewe and carried a plaque to that effect. Four engines survived into preservation. The examples built after nationalisation included BR Standard features, common to 'Class 2' 2-6-2T, 84000 types.

The final Ivatt design was also a 'Mogul' type but a much bigger and more powerful machine than his 'twins' with a striking appearance, which earned the class the ungracious nickname 'Flying Pig'. The Ivatt 2-6-0 'Class 4MT' locomotives were designed to replace aging freight types but in practice were found to be equally at home hauling passenger services. The utilisation of a high running plate completely exposing the cylinders, wheels and frames gave the type an American look, somewhat reminiscent of the USA Austerity S160 Class.

Ivatt designed the class with a view to easy maintenance and like his Class 2s the 4MTs were fitted with rocking grates, self-cleaning smokeboxes, self-emptying ashpans and cut-away tender sides. The first 50 of the class (43000 to 43049) were built with double chimney/blast pipes which instead of improving performance actually impaired steam generation. After converting back to single chimney/blast pipes the engine's boilers produced over double the amount of steam, and the remaining locomotives were built in that fashion. As modified the Ivatt Mogul 4MTs performed well in service and the type found their way to all corners of the network being popular engines with both footplate and maintenance crews. First examples entered service in December 1947; the first of the class was withdrawn in December 1963 with eight examples lasting until the end of BR steam. ■

BUILD DETAILS IVATT 2-6-0 CLASS 4MT, 162 LOCOMOTIVES BUILT		
Horwich	43000-43049	1947 to 1949
Doncaster	43050-43069	1950
Darlington	43070-43106	1950 to 1951
Doncaster	43107-43111	1951
Horwich	43112-43136	1951 to 1952
Doncaster	43137-43161	1951 to 1952

One member of the class 43106 survived into preservation. Examples built after nationalisation included BR Standard features, common to 'Class 4' 2-6-0, 76000 types.

British Steam

Right: **Preserved Ivatt 4MT 43106 is seen on Welsh Marches Pullman duty with ex- GWR 4-6-0 Erlestoke Manor in June 1982.**

Below: **Double-headed Ivatt 'Twins' 41312 and 46521 are seen in restored condition at 'Waterworks Crossing' on the Severn Valley Railway.**

BR STANDARD LOCOMOTIVES
AND RA RIDDLES

As the rundown railways of Britain struggled to recover from the forced neglect and generally debilitating after-effects of WWII, the lack of modern motive power was uppermost in the minds of those charged with overseeing the creation of British Railways in January 1948. Although the embryonic British Transport Commission was well aware of the growing trend towards dieselisation and electrification in other parts of the world and also the rapidly expanding road transport industry in the UK, they chose to build a range of modern steam locomotives.

Experimental diesel types were introduced during the same period but the short to medium term strategy was to replace the 'life expired' steam locomotives, inherited by BR from the 'big four', with a fleet of easily maintained efficient replacements. In order to achieve the post-war desired steam renaissance BR, under the guidance of the BTC, selected Robert Arthur Riddles as being the man to get the job done. However industry insiders and civil servants (including Dr Richard Beeching) at the BTC foresaw a long term future without steam for BR!

Like so many other great locomotive engineers Riddles served an apprenticeship at LNWR Crewe Works. He became a locomotive fitter at Rugby until called to serve in WWI. After completing war service Riddles returned to Rugby for a time until in 1920 he was appointed as Assistant to the Works Manager at Crewe. When HG Ivatt was appointed to the post of Works Superintendent Derby in 1928 Riddles became his assistant. Interestingly the pair oversaw the production of the second batch of Fowler Royal Scot 4-6-0s at Derby.

Riddles returned to Crewe in 1931, this time to work as assistant to William A Stanier, until in a 1937 'job swap' he went to St Rollox Glasgow as Electrical and Mechanical Engineer Scotland and Ivatt returned to Crewe as first assistant to Stanier. Riddles was heavily involved with the Coronation Scot project and even 'footplated' 6220 'Coronation' at the time of the 114mph record run. In a continuance of his association with the 'Coronation Scot' he made the trip to the USA with the 1939 exhibition train and when driver Fred Bishop became ill he ended up driving the train for most of the tour. At the onset of WWII Riddles was seconded to the newly formed Directorate of Transportation Equipment; a

consequence of that appointment was his involvement with the building of Austerity locomotives.

He returned to the LMS in 1943 as Chief Stores Superintendent and in that year received a CBE for his wartime services. After the unexpected death of Fairburn (Stanier's successor) Ivatt was appointed as LMS CME, a job which Riddles thought that he should have been given. But he was not disappointed for long being promoted himself shortly after to Vice-President of the LMS, and thus effectively Ivatt's boss! Nationalisation of the railways saw Riddles (a Member of the Railway Executive for Mechanical and Electrical Engineering) given a role similar to that of Chief Mechanical Engineer for the newly formed British Railways.

Although Riddles is credited with being the man who designed and oversaw the building of the 999 new locomotives, which became collectively known as BR Standards, it should be remembered that he was very much the leader of a talented team. He was more than ably assisted by Ernest Stewart Cox who was the chairman of the 'standards committee' charged with collecting information from draughtsmen and engineers around the BR regions.

Left: **The last steam locomotive built by British Railways was Standard 9F 2-10-0, 92220 'Evening Star'. It is seen here in preservation at Delamere CLC in 1985 with a 'White Rose' working.**

Standard 'Class 5' 5MT 4-6-0 is seen at 70B Feltham (70B) as the crew prepare to drop the ashes. This Swindon built loco was withdrawn in 1967.

THE BRITANNIA CLASS.

The first 'BR Standard' No 70000 'Britannia' was unveiled in January 1951; it was the first of 55 members of the 'Class 7' 7MT 4-6-2 types, all were built at Crewe between 1951 and 1954. The number series was 70000-70054 and all but one, 70047, were named. Loco 70004 'William Shakespeare' was exhibited at the 1954 Festival of Britain and thereafter allocated to Stewarts Lane (73A) specifically to work the prestigious 'Golden Arrow' service.

The Britannia's design was generally considered to be a complete success, and originally members of the class were allocated to all parts of BR. In the early days the type put in some memorable performances on the former Great Eastern Railway main line into East Anglia, as a result of which timings were appreciably improved.

As dieselisation (and later electrification) became more advanced all of the Britannias were transferred to the London Midland Region. The first to be scrapped was 70007 'Coeur-de-Lion' which was cut up at Crewe in July 1965, having worked in BR service for only 14 years. By 1966 just 42 of the class were still in use and only one loco 70013 'Oliver Cromwell' worked into 1968. Two of the class 70000 'Britannia' and 70013 'Oliver Cromwell' survived into preservation.

THE 'DUKE'

Those, who in later times, restored it to running order proudly declare that not only is Standard 8P 71000 'Duke of Gloucester' the 'one and only' it is the ultimate steam locomotive! In its new life that may well be the case. But those who crewed the 1954-built loco in BR service would perhaps only acquiesce to the first part of the claim. Information collated from performance reports over the eight years and six months which 71000 spent on the main line suggest that the three-cylinder 8P Pacific was anything but the ultimate steam locomotive.

As the modernisation programme was well under way at the time it seemed that BR were not minded to allocate resources for research into the reported draughting problems associated with the big engine. With hindsight, and after a great deal of the work, the members of the 71000 Trust claim to have proved what Riddles was unable to, the 8P 4-6-2 is, they say, 'now the world's most advanced steam locomotive'. The Crewe-built engine's main line performances in preservation seem to confirm the 'ultimate' claim. The Standard 'Class 8' has been in preservation since 1974 and has steamed considerably longer in private ownership than it did for BR.

Above: **Britannia Class 7MT 4-6-2, 70032 'Tennyson' (minus nameplates and smokebox number plate) prepares to leave Preston with a southbound service in September 1966. 'Tennyson' was withdrawn in September 1967 and cut up six months later.** *Roger Jermy.*

Below: **Britannia Class 7MT 4-6-2 Standard 70015 'Apollo' (note the nameplates are missing) is seen being serviced in this 1960s picture. The footplate man shovelling out the ash from the smokebox can just be seen.**

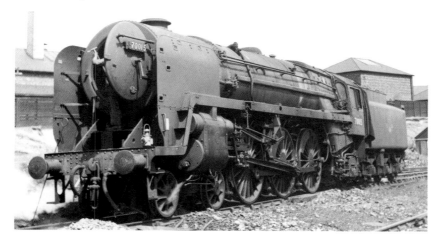

THE CLANS

Between 1951 and 1952 ten lighter versions of the Britannia class were constructed, they were the Standard 'Class 6' 6MT 4-6-2 Clans. However the Crewe-built small Pacifics were not as successful as their bigger cousins and that fact coupled with the quickening pace of dieselisation caused an order for a further 15 to be cancelled. All of the class were allocated to the Scottish Region and worked mainly on Glasgow-Manchester/Liverpool express services. Locomotives numbered 72000-72004 were taken out of service in 1962, numbers 72005, 72007 and 72009 in 1965 while 72006 and 72008 lasted until 1966. None were preserved.

STANDARD 4-6-0s

The BR Standard Doncaster-designed 'Class 5' 5MT 4-6-0 types were produced between 1951 and 1957 and the 172 locomotives given the number series 73000-73171. They were based on the LMS type 'Black Fives' and intended to replace that class, the LNER type B1s, the GWR type Halls and the SR type King Arthur Class. The Class 5s were sent to all regions of BR and 20 of the SR allocation were given the names of the 'Arthurs' they replaced. In line with all the Standard types which followed, they were successful engines, incorporating cut-away tender sides to improve vision when running tender first. The Standards were easier to maintain and service, being fitted with standard self-cleaning features. Locomotives 73125-54 were fitted with Caprotti valve gear. Five examples were preserved.

The BR Standard Brighton-designed 'Class 4' 4MT 4-6-0 types were also produced between 1951 and 1957 and the 80 locomotives were given the number series 75000-75079. All of the class were built at Swindon Works and numbers 75066-75079 were fitted with double chimneys. Being smaller and lighter than the 5MTs they had greater route availability and were to be seen over all of the BR system. Six examples were preserved.

Above: **Doncaster 1957 built Standard 'Class 5' 5MT 4-6-0, 73171 is seen receiving the attention of a fitter, while the footplate crew look on. Pictured at Nine Elms (70A) in July 1966, this loco served BR for nine years and five months.**

BUILD DETAILS OF THE STANDARD 'CLASS 5' 4-6-0:

Derby Works	73000-73099 and 73125-73154
Doncaster Works	73100-73124 and 73155-73171

Above: **Built at Crewe in 1951-1952 the 6MT BR Standard 'Clan' Class 4-6-2, 72003 'Clan Fraser' is pictured on a Liverpool/Manchester – Glasgow Central express nearing Beattock Summit. This loco was withdrawn by BR in December 1962.**
David Anderson.

Below: **Night Mail! Derby-built BR Standard 'Class 5' 4-6-0, 73011 waits while mailbags are unloaded at Liverpool Exchange Station (closed April 1977). This time-exposure picture was taken in August 1966, 73011 was withdrawn a year later.**
Roger Jermy.

Britannia Class 7MT 4-6-2, 70013 'Oliver Cromwell' was the last steam locomotive to be overhauled at Crewe Works. It is pictured there on 27 November 1965.

BR Standard 'Class 4' 2-6-0, 76001 is seen on Beattock near Harthope with a northbound freight on 8 July 1959. Note the '08' diesel being towed dead in the train. 76001 was built at Horwich in 1952 and withdrawn in August 1966, then stored out of use for a while before being scrapped in March 1968. *David Anderson*

STANDARD MOGULS

The Doncaster-designed 'Standard Class 4' 4MT 2-6-0 types were built between 1952 and 1957. The 'Class 4' Moguls were based on the earlier Ivatt '4300 Class' 2-6-0s and were intended for cross-country work, they were used successfully on a wide variety of duties. The class were allocated to all BR regions except the Western Region; four examples were preserved.

Below: **BR Standard 'Class 3' 3MT 2-6-0, 77012 is attracting the attention of visiting enthusiasts at Eaglescliffe in September 1955. The 'Mogul' was Swindon built and entered service in June 1954; serving BR for 13 years it was withdrawn in June 1967.**

BUILD DETAILS OF THE STANDARD 'CLASS 4' 2-6-0:

Horwich Works	76000-76019 and 76075-76099
Doncaster Works	76020-76074 and 76100-76114

BR Standard 'Class 2' 2MT Mogul is pictured on shed at Bangor MPD (6H formerly 7B) in 1963. The depot closed in 1965 and Darlington-built 78003 was withdrawn from Shrewsbury (84G) by BR in December 1966.

In 1954 Swindon Works designed and produced 20 locomotives of the 'Standard Class 3' 3MT 2-6-0 type and they were effectively the twins of the 82000 series tank engines with the number series 77000-77019. These locomotives were allocated (when new) to the Eastern Region, North Eastern Region and the Scottish Region. An order for a further five of these locos was placed but then cancelled. None were preserved.

The Derby-designed 'Standard Class 2' 2MT 2-6-0 types with the number series 78000-78064 were similar in design to the Ivatt LMS 4MT '46400' types. All 65 of this very popular class, designed for light passenger work, were built at Darlington Works between 1952 and 1956. The '84000' tank class was the twin of this design. Four examples were preserved.

British Steam

Standard tank 'Class 4' 4MT. 80043 was a regular S&D engine which was withdrawn from Templecombe (83G) in March 1966. The 1964 location is Exeter St David's and a permanent way ballast train, being banked by an unidentified loco. The SR disc 'head-code' indicates a Bournemouth Central-Dorchester goods train.

STANDARD TANKS

The '80000' series was the first of three Riddles Standard tank locomotive types. The 'Class 4' 4MT 2-6-4T was a highly successful design which when allocated to all regions of BR, except the Western, found universal favour with engine crews. There were 155 built between 1951 and 1957. The Brighton design incorporated the same boiler as the Standard 4MT tender engines. Only 25 of these locomotives lasted until 1966 and none made it past the end of 1967. Fifteen examples of the class were preserved.

The 'Standard Class 3' 3MT 2-6-2Ts, with the number series 82000-82044, were all built at Swindon Works between 1952 and 1955 and were intended for light passenger work. Based on the GWR '6100 Class' they were further developed to become the Class 3MT, 77000 series tender engines. BR allocated all 45 of this class to the Southern and Western Regions. None were preserved.

The third Standard tank type was the Derby-designed 'Standard Class 2' 2MT 2-6-2T with the number series 84000-84029; they were the tank version of the 78000 series tender engines. All the class were intended for light passenger duties and were fitted for 'push and pull' working. The first 20 built 84000- 84019 were allocated to the London Midland Region and the final 10 84020-84029 to the Southern Region. Loco number 84020 was taken to Eastleigh Works with the intention of converting it for use (then trialling it) on the Isle of Wight, with a plan for other engines of the type to be later allocated to Ryde (71F) but the plan never came to fruition. None were preserved.

Crewe-built Standard tank 84001 'Class 2' 2MT 2-6-2T was withdrawn from Llandudno Junction (6G) in 1964, it is pictured there on 26 May 1963.

BR Standard tank locomotive 'Class 3' 3MT 2-6-2T is seen outside the running shed at Chester in August 1958. This Swindon-built engine was withdrawn by BR in July 1965 and 'cut' four months later.

BUILD DETAILS OF THE STANDARD 'CLASS 2' 2-6-2T:

Crewe	84000-84019
Darlington	84020-84029

THE MIGHTY 9Fs

By far most powerful, and many would argue the most successful BR Standard type was the 'Class 9F' 2-10-0, Brighton-designed freight locomotives. Engine number 92220 holds the distinction of being the last steam locomotive built by British Railways, painted in lined green livery and given a GWR style copper-topped chimney; it was rolled out of Swindon Works in March 1960, and to mark the occasion was named 'Evening Star'.

This impressive class had only a short service life, but long enough to prove their worth. The original design 9F 2-10-0s were powerful, reliable and popular with the engine crews. The 21ft 8in wheelbase had to be capable of following tight curves and, to achieve this, the team designed the centre pair of driving wheels without flanges, and to widen route availability kept the axle loading to only 15 tons 10cwt. The locomotives were designed for use on the heaviest of freight trains at reasonably high speeds. In service they also worked passenger trains at speeds reported to be between 80 and 90mph, an incredible achievement for an engine with only 5ft diameter driving wheels.

Real pulling power was the main asset of the Standard Class 9s. With great success they worked heavy, mineral, coal and general freight trains. The Tyne Dock-Consett workings were perhaps the hardest regular tasks ever undertaken by the class, and those iron ore trains could weigh up to 787 tons each. In addition they had to be hauled up gradients as steep as 1-in-35, a task that proved well within the capabilities of 9Fs working in pairs. Ten examples 92060-92066 and 92097-92099 were fitted with

Westinghouse air pumps in order to work the hopper doors on the mineral trains. Nine of the original-build Standard 9F 2-10-0s survived into preservation

BUILD DETAILS OF THE STANDARD 'CLASS 9F' 2-10-0:

Crewe	92000-92019	1954
Crewe	92020-92029	built as Franco Crosti types 1955
Crewe	92030-92086	1954/56
Swindon	92087-92096	1956/57
Crewe	92097-92177	1956/58
Swindon	92178-92220	1959/60
Crewe	92221-92250	1958

THE FRANCO-CROSTI EXPERIMENT

In 1955 the design team experimented unsuccessfully with the Franco Crosti boiler system, to hopefully save on coal and also make lower-quality coal usable. The resultant twin boiler locomotives had smaller fireboxes and conventional tapered boilers 'on' the frames, located above pre-heat boilers 'between' the frames. Each boiler had a separate smokebox door. Draughting and exhaust systems were altered accordingly. The 9F Crosti venture was unsuccessful and therefore abandoned in 1958. The 10 engines were then converted to conventional operation (the pre-heat boiler was retained but sealed off). Because of their smaller firebox and boiler they were reclassified to 8F, retaining their Crosti look they were not fitted with smoke deflectors. ■

Above: **BR Standard 'Class 4' 4MT 4-6-0, 75048 (again minus smokebox number plate) blasts through Caergwrle Castle Station on 11 March 1967. This Swindon-built locomotive served BR until February 1967.**

Right: **The smokebox number plate has already been removed from Standard 'Class5' 5MT 4-6-0, 73169! It is seen at Raynes Park in June 1966 and was withdrawn from Eastleigh (70D) in the October of that year.**

BRITISH RAILWAYS STANDARD 9F 2-10-0 VARIANTS

92050 is pictured at Toton shed (18A) in 1958. This Standard 9F was built at Crewe and entered BR service in August 1955. Compared with other members of the class 92050 had a reasonably long service life being withdrawn in September 1967. For example preserved loco 92220 'Evening Star' only served BR from March 1960 until March 1965, sister Swindon-built loco 92210 managed just five years and three months before being withdrawn. This loco was a 'normal' BR 9F build, as are all nine of the preserved examples.

Pictured near Chester in 1958 in 'as built' Franco Crosti form is 92028. The engine's conventional chimney was used only on 'light up' and the exhaust exited via a multiple blast pipe and long thin chimney (under the odd-looking smoke deflector) on the side of the locomotive. Note the two smokebox doors.

BR Standard Crosti 2-10-0, 92022 seen after being converted back to normal draughting, the 'down' power rated 2-10-0 freight locomotive is seen in 1967 at Stockport, with a train of chemical tanks. 92022 was withdrawn in November 1967. Note that the smokebox door of the lower preheat boiler has been replaced by a conventional step.

Standard 9Fs in the number series 92183-92250 were either built with, or later given, double chimneys. 92219 is pictured at Southall (81C) in 1964. Sorry about the post in front of the rear of the tender. Those who ever tried it will confirm, it wasn't always easy getting the shot you wanted when creeping around a shed yard on a Sunday afternoon, and attempting to avoid the duty foreman!

A summer scene at Lancaster Castle with two 9Fs crossing. Note the 60s family and in particular the fact that the little girl is covering her ears, delightful!

When photographed heading south at Moore (WCML) in May 1967 Crewe-built Standard 9F 2-10-0, 92133 had only two months left in BR service. The loco was withdrawn in July of that year and cut up in January of the following year, having served BR for 10 years and two months.

Standard 9F 2-10-0 92233 is seen with a mineral train near Blea Moor Signalbox (S&C) in August 1965. This Crewe-built loco entered service in August 1958 and was withdrawn by BR in February 1968, service life nine years and six months.

WAR DEPARTMENT
AUSTERITY LOCOMOTIVES

In September 1939 RA Riddles was appointed to the newly created position of Director of Transportation Equipment for the Ministry of Supply, on the very day that war broke out between Britain and Germany. He was given a comprehensive role which included overseeing the manufacture of diverse items of equipment all seen as essential to the war effort; the list included 'Bailey bridges', cranes, Mulberry harbours and even jerricans! As far as the railways were concerned his brief was clear, large numbers of locomotives were needed to help the war effort; he had to select or create the type(s) and, while being mindful of the impending scarcity of raw material and resources, get them built quickly.

His first thought was to repeat the emergency actions taken during WWI and make available quantities of Robinson GCR-designed 2-8-0s to the military. Among his reasons for discounting that possibility was their excessive width (over the outside cylinders) which restricted route availability. The War Department had already placed an order for 240 Stanier 8Fs which should have been shipped to France, but the retreat from Dunkirk put paid to that plan, the Stanier 8Fs were redirected to other theatres of war where they performed with distinction.

The Ministry of Supply had already selected a shunting locomotive design to complement the fleet of Wartime General Duties Locomotives which Riddles was asked to create, that loco was a powerful 'Austerity' 0-6-0ST originated by the Hunslet Engine Company, which Riddles' design team modified to suit WD requirements. The Saddle tank had the look of a traditional industrial locomotive but was in all respects a 'big' little engine. With a power rating of 4F the Austerity tank, which had 4ft 3in diameter driving wheels, justified universal route availability.

The Hunslet/Riddles 0-6-0ST was built in great numbers between 1943 and 1946 by not only the Hunslet Engine Co Ltd but by Andrew Barclay Sons & Co Ltd, WG Bagnall Ltd, Hudwell Clarke & Co Ltd, Robert Stephenson & Hawthorns Ltd and Vulcan Foundry Ltd. From the several hundred built many were sold at the end of the war to industrial concerns, docks, mines, steel works etc, in addition the LNER bought 75 of the engines (numbered them as 8006-8080) with the class identity 'J94'. In 1948 they became British Railways stock with the number series 68006-68080. The design proved ideal for preserved railways and about 50 examples survived to work again, including two of the LNER batch, numbers 68077 and 68078.

The accuracy of the word 'Austerity' as applied to the WD engines is easily explained by the examination of a few facts. The Stanier 2-8-0 8Fs used approximately 22 tons of steel castings per engine while the WD 2-8-0 8Fs were constructed using only 2½ tons of steel castings. For example cast iron was used for the cylinders, blast pipe, smokebox saddle, chimney and front-end cylinder covers. Parallel boilers and round-topped fireboxes were a far cheaper option than the Stanier tapered boiler and Belpaire firebox. North British Locomotive Ltd assembled the first WD 2-8-0 in only 10 working days, thus creating a record for the firm when the first WD 8F was outshopped on 16 January 1943. Records show that the 'Austerities' were built at almost twice the rate at which it had been possible to build the Stanier 8F.

Between 1943 and 1946 a total of 934 WD 2-8-0 MOD (WD) 'Austerity' locomotives were built by North British Locomotive Co Ltd and Vulcan Foundry Ltd. Many saw service in France, Belgium and Holland during WWII. `

Main pic: **WD 2-8-0 8F number 90733 is seen under test at LNWR Heritage Crewe after a 2007 restoration to working condition. This loco was WD 79257, it worked in Holland as number 4464 and then in Sweden as number 1931. The BR number it carries in restoration is a fictitious one, as the BR number series ended at 90732.**

Left: **Built by Vulcan Foundry in 1944 WD 8F 2-8-0 No 90624 is pictured on an 'Up' Motherwell-Carlisle freight on 18 April 1959. This locomotive was withdrawn by BR in September 1962 and was from the ex-LNER batch.**
David Anderson.

The sheer size of the Hunslet type WD 'Austerity' 0-6-0ST can be gauged in this picture of the beautifully restored example 68030 when seen coupled to ex-GWR 2-8-0T 5224, at the Churnet Valley Railway. The number given to the 0-6-0ST is simply representative of the engine it portrays as the Hunslet Engine Co Ltd-built loco which carried that BR number was scrapped in October 1962. The present 68030 is a restored WD engine which was in private ownership.

From delivery until October 1944 all the 2-8-0s in service were 'loaned' by the WD to the UK railway companies but starting in November of that year WD 8F locomotives were gradually shipped to mainland Europe, additionally in 1946 twelve of the class were shipped 'out east' to work on the Kowloon-Canton Railway.

In 1947 the LNER purchased 200 of the type which they relisted as their class '07'. BR had 533 of the type on loan from the WD at the time of nationalisation which they purchased before the end of 1948, and renumbered in 1949. The BR number series was 90000-90421 (ex-NBL engines) 90422-90732 (ex-VF engines). Locomotive number 90732 (WD number 79312) carried the name 'Vulcan'. None of the UK-based WD 8Fs survived, all being scrapped before 1967; however a loco of the type repatriated from Europe (WD number 79257) is preserved in the UK.

There was, in 1943, a bigger version of the WD Austerity 8F built by the North British Locomotive Company, with a 2-10-0 wheel arrangement. That class of 150 locomotives were given the extra set of wheels in order to allow them to work over lighter laid track. One of the MOD WD 'Austerity' 8F class 2-10-0s (WD number 73755) had the distinction of being the 1000th WD loco built in the UK and shipped to Europe since D-Day, it was named 'Longmoor' by the military.

In 1944 a batch of 20 of the 2-10-0s were shipped to the Middle East, a further 103 were sent to the Low Countries during 1944/45. That left 25 of the class working in the UK (mostly in Scotland) plus two examples in military use. BR purchased the 25 UK-based WD 8F 2-10-0s in 1948, numbering them 90750-90774. Numbers 90773 and 90774 both carried the name, 'North British'; the names were removed by BR c1952. All of the class were withdrawn before the end of 1962. No ex-BR examples were preserved, but loco number 600 'Gordon' from the Longmoor Military Railway was. ■

WG Bagnall Ltd-built ex-WD 0-6-0ST shunter, seen as BR 68057 (LNER 8057) at West Hartlepool (51C) in 1960.

WD 8F 2-10-0 number 90762 is seen hard at work on Beattock Bank. Loco 90762 was built by NBL in July 1945 and withdrawn by BR in December 1962.

Above: The Railway Operating Division of the Royal Engineers (ROD) adopted the Robinson-designed GCR Class 04 2-8-0 locomotives to use as 'their' engine of war in WWI, 521 of the class were built by various companies for service in France and in WWII 92 of the engines were commandeered to work in Egypt and Palestine. GCR/ROD 2-8-0 7F, 63647 is pictured at Doncaster (36A).

Ex-Lancashire & Yorkshire Railway Aspinal-designed Class '21' 0-4-0ST 'Pugs' c1900. Seen in 1997 just before the closure of the steam centre at Southport which operated from the town's ex-L&YR, LMS and later BR depot, the saddle tank locomotives pictured are 51231 and 51218 respectively. But all is not what it seems; unserviceable locomotive 51231 is in reality ex-L&Y No 19 (LMS 11243) which was sold out of service by the LMS in 1931. Loco 51218 was in working order, but the smoke effect on 51231 was a special effect. Coal was carried inside the cab of these specialist dock shunters, note also the dumb buffers (wooden blocks).

TANK LOCOMOTIVES

As an alternative to carrying coal and water in a separate (but attached) vehicle (like tender types), tank locomotives were constructed with integral coal bunkers and water tanks. Doing so made for cheaper manufacturing costs but brought with it a restriction on miles travelled between water and coal replenishment. Normally the range from its base of a tank locomotive would have been no further than 20 miles making them suitable for branch line work or shunting, but in the main unsuitable for long distance express passenger work. A notable exception were the 2-6-4T LMS and BR-built engines which carried 2000 gallons of water and 3½ tons of coal, they were quite capable of working passenger routes of 50 miles in distance.

Adams Radial Tank 4-4-2T, No 488 'Class 415', this venerable preserved engine became a centenarian in 1985. It was built for the LSWR by Neilson & Co Ltd in 1885; 488 became a military engine in 1919 after which it was sold to the privately run East Kent Railway. In 1946 the SR bought it and, after an overhaul, sent it to work on the Lyme Regis Branch. It was withdrawn from there by BR in 1961 and is now preserved. Numbers carried: 488, 0488, EKR 5, 3488, 30583.

Not all stations had motive power depots, and not all MPDs had turntables, hence tank engines were ideal for operating trains on such routes because they could safely be worked 'bunker first'. Furthermore apart from the early 'half cab' versions tank locos gave the footplate crews good protection from the elements. With numerous urban areas of high population density requiring train services over relatively short distances the UK network was perfect tank loco territory. Many and varied types passed into BR ownership from the 'Big Four'.

The three most common types of tank locomotive design are: Saddle Tank, where the water is carried in a curved tank wrapped around the top of the boiler; Side Tank, where the water is carried in tanks mounted on the locomotive's frames on either side of the boiler, and Pannier Tanks (famously favoured by the GWR) where rounded cornered rectangular tanks on each side of the

BR Standard 2-6-2T 'Class 3 Tank' 82013 is pictured between duties at Waterloo in 1966. This 1952 Swindon-built loco was withdrawn in June 1964.

Although a traditional GWR-style pannier tank, 1669 was built by British Railways at Swindon in 1955. The 0-6-0PT Hawksworth 2F '16xx Class' is pictured at Wolverhampton in 1958. This loco was withdrawn after 10 years service with BR, and subsequently scrapped in February 1966.

loco are mounted flush with the top of the boiler. In almost all those examples the coal was carried in a rear bunker, which often had an additional water storage space built into the bottom of it. A less common type of tank locomotive design is the Well Tank, where the water is carried in tanks between the locomotive's frames. The most numerous type of wheel arrangement for tank locomotives taken into BR stock was 0-6-0.

Operational tank locomotives taken into BR stock in 1948, totalled (all types) some 7411. Their origins were ex-GWR 2387 locomotives, ex-SR 647 locomotives, ex-LMS 2198 locomotives and ex-LNER 2179 locomotives. The Ivatt 2MT types built after 1948 increased the stock by 100 engines and the BR Standard building programme (after 1951) added a further 230. However the withdrawal of older types was by then well under way. In BR steam 'mid term' (1958) 5359 tank locomotives remained in service, but by the end of 1967 all had been withdrawn. ∎

Ex-LSWR Drummond 1899 Nine Elms-built 'M7 Class' 0-4-4T, 30023 pictured at Exeter St David's Station in 1958 while double heading with an unidentified SR Mogul. This loco was withdrawn by BR in October 1961 and cut up a month later.

Above: BR Standard 2-6-4 'Class 4 Tank' 80141 is seen stored out of use at Nine Elms (70A) on 5 March 1966, note the side rods have been removed. The loco was withdrawn from traffic in December 1966 and scrapped four weeks later.

Right: Ex-GWR Modified '45xx Class' 5541 is a preserved locomotive. It is seen waiting to depart Barmouth (former Cambrian Railway) in May 1953.

Left: Note the extra coal carried on the cab roof of this ex-LNER 0-6-0T J72. Locos in this class were built to the orders of three different railway companies, the North Eastern Railway 1898-1923, the LNER 1925 and by BR 1948-1951. No 68750 was built at Doncaster in 1925 and withdrawn by BR in December 1962, but not cut up until February 1964. Pictured shunting at Motherwell Morningside (66B) in 1961.

TAKING WATER

Above: **Water at speed. Princess Coronation 46222 'Queen Mary' takes water while in charge of the 'up' Royal Scot train. Pictured at Strawfrank Junction Troughs on the WCML, in 1958. Note the spray emanating from the scoop located under the tender.**
David Anderson

Right: **A conventional platform located water tower fed by a header tank is being used to fill this ex-GWR locomotive.**

On nearly all long-distance express journeys the rostered steam locomotives, if in good condition, could complete their tasks without having to replenish coal supplies, but water was a different issue altogether. Even though coal consumption figures would vary greatly from loco to loco depending on how hard or otherwise it was worked, the engine would almost always get safely to the end of its run. Water usage also varied widely and standing unexpectedly at red signals etc did not help the cause.

It was common practice for locomotive crews to take water at scheduled stops along the route and on a long haul that could be necessary on several occasions. It was possible for a freight train to make extra water stops if needed but passenger trains had to run to timetables. Express locomotive tenders varied in size, and thus capacity, the following table gives some idea of the averages.

Water was taken from conventional lineside water towers the design of which varied according to the railway company; they were usually located at platform ends and within motive power depots. In order to minimise the number of water stops during express passenger services the railway companies came up with the idea of putting water-filled troughs between the metals on straight lengths of track.

While travelling over the troughs at speed the locomotive fireman was able to lower a scoop, connected to the tender, into the trough. The forward motion of the train then forced water up the shoot and into the tender. The resultant spray made a fine spectacle but the system worked well; at one point BR had over 140 such troughs. A typical length of trough was 600 yards but several were built up to a half a mile in length.

The steel trough sections were 18in wide and could accommodate water up to a depth of 5in; they were manufactured in 14ft sections. At a speed of between 40 and 50mph a locomotive could pick up about 2000 gallons of water. The water in the troughs was of course susceptible to frost and in an attempt to overcome that the Great Central Railway incorporated steam pipes in their troughs. ■

LOCO TYPE	COAL CAPACITY	WATER CAPACITY
GWR 'Castle' Class	6 tons	3500 gallons
GWR 'King' Class	6 tons	4000 gallons
LMS 'Princess Royal' Class	10 tons	4000 gallons
LMS 'Princess Coronation' Class	10 tons	4000 gallons
SR 'Merchant Navy' Class	5 tons	5100 gallons
LMS 'Black Five' Class	9 tons	4000 gallons
LNER 'B1' Class	7.5 tons	4200 gallons
LNER 'A4' Class	9 tons	5000 gallons
'Britannia' Class	7/9 tons	4250/5000 gallons

Above: **The fireman is watching the tender tank fill in this picture taken at Trafford Park MPD (9E).**

Left: **Princess Coronation 46221 'Queen Elizabeth' is taking water at Strawfrank Troughs while in charge of a 'down' Birmingham-Glasgow service.**
David Anderson.

A TRIO OF **A4 PACIFICS**

Top: Gresley A4 4-6-2, 60009 'Union of South Africa' is seen in preservation carrying the name she was intended to have but was never given 'Osprey', pictured in 1991 with a North Wales Coast Express.

Right: Gresley A4 4-6-2, 60034 'Lord Farringdon' pictured at York Station in 1960.

Below: Gresley A4 4-6-2 4498 (LNER number) Sir Nigel Gresley is pictured in preservation with The Western Jubilee excursion in 1977.

A TRIO OF **A1 PACIFICS**

Top: A1 8P 4-6-2 60162 'Saint Johnstoun' is pictured passing Haymarket MPD with a Waverley-Aberdeen express in the summer of 1956. *David Anderson.*

Left: A1 8P 4-6-2 60114 'WP Allen' is pictured leaving the coaling plant at York in 1964.

Below: A1 8P 4-6-2 60152 'Holyrood' easing off Haymarket depot is seen at Haymarket Central Junction in September 1957. The Edinburgh-Glasgow lines are in the foreground with access tracks to depot on the left. Over the main line is the former Caledonian Railway Edinburgh (Princes Street) to Granton and Leith route (now removed). *David Anderson.*

Perth Station in July 1964 and Gresley 2-6-2 'V2 Class',
60919 has just arrived double headed with the 'then' future, D6105. The
V2 was withdrawn in September 1966 having steamed for 25 years. The diesel, a
member of the less than successful 'Class 21', had a much shorter lifespan, it was built by North
British Locomotive for BR in 1958 and withdrawn from Eastfield (65A) in June 1968! Begging the question
with this double pairing, who was helping who?

THE SCOTTISH SCENE

The Scottish Region of British Railways formed in January 1948 was created from elements of the post-grouping LNER and LMS. The LMS alphanumeric system of locomotive shed identification was nationally adopted at that time and thus several changes were made in order to take into account the system, and accommodate regionalisation. For example the ex-LMS loco shed at Inverness changed from 31A to 60A, while the code for the ex-LNER depot at Thornton changed from THJ to 62A.

60919 and D6105 are pictured at Perth having been detached from the stock.

There were 44 Scottish Region steam depots at the onset of BR and the principal ones were: Inverness (60A), Kittybrewster (61A), Thornton (62A), Perth (63A), St Margaret's (64A), Eastfield (65A), Polmadie (66A), Corkerhill (67A) and Carlisle Kingmoor (68A).

The principal intercity station in Edinburgh is the world famous Waverley Station which serves the East Coast Main Line and stations to the north; there has been a railway facility on that site since 1846. Edinburgh Princes Street Station was a departure point for numerous steam services including a frequent service to Glasgow, that station closed in 1966. The principal main line station in Glasgow is Central Station which opened in 1879 and is the Scottish terminus for the West Coast Main Line; Glasgow Queen Street Station, which opened in 1845, still serves inter-regional trains to almost all parts of Scotland.

Under nationalisation four locomotive works became part of BR Scottish Region. Cowlairs

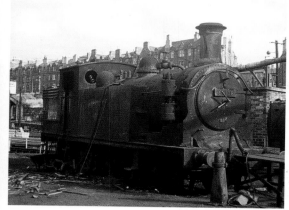

Still of use. Reid North British 0-6-2T 'N15' Class is seen as a stationary boiler at St Margaret's Depot Edinburgh in August 1964.

North British Locomotive Co Ltd-built Reid 'Class J37' No 64569 dating from 1914 is pictured in 1957 leaving Inverkeithing with an excursion to the Fife Coast. *David Anderson.*

Ex-LNER B1 4-6-0 61076 is pictured outside Edinburgh Waverley Station in August 1964.

Gresley A4 Pacific 60019 Bittern (a preserved loco) is pictured approaching Perth with an Aberdeen service in 1963.

Locomotive Works was built to serve the Edinburgh & Glasgow Railway and it opened in 1842. The first locomotives constructed in 1844 were a pair of 0-6-0WT 'Well Tanks' built specifically to work the Cowlairs Incline. In 1886 Cowlairs became the main works for the North British Railway, and in 1923 part of the newly formed LNER. The last locomotives built were Reid Class N15 0-6-2Ts and they brought the number of Cowlairs-built engines up to approximately 850. Under BR the works continued to carry out locomotive repair work and closed in 1968.

Inverurie Works was one of the most northerly loco works and service depots in the UK, it was opened in 1903 to serve the Great North of Scotland Railway. The first locomotive was built in 1909 and the last and 10th in 1921. The facility continued as a repair shop and in 1955 was reconfigured to accommodate larger locomotives (BR Standards). BR engines continued to be repaired on the site until its closure on New Year's Eve 1969. Kilmarnock Locomotive Works was built in 1856 for the Glasgow & South Western Railway Company. In 1921 the last and 392nd locomotive was built at Kilmarnock, in 1923 it became part of the LMSR. After becoming a BR asset it became a repair facility but lost that status in 1952, completely closing in 1959.

St Rollox Locomotive Works was opened by the Caledonian Railway in 1853. In 1854 the first steam locomotive, a 2-4-0 was completed and the last steam locomotive was built in 1928, it was an 0-6-0 numbered 4476. A total of approximately 500 St Rollox-built steam locomotives made it into BR service although over 20 were almost immediately withdrawn. The list included 23 examples of the celebrated 'Dunalastair IV Class' 4-4-0s, almost 200 Drummond 'Jumbo Class' 0-6-0s and 27 McIntosh '812 Class' 0-6-0s including 57566, a preserved example. The aging St Rollox locomotives were steadily 'culled' by BR throughout the 50s and 60s, but records show that some carried on working until the end of 1963. None survived in service until the end of steam on BR. The works (by then a repair shop) was renamed Glasgow Works in 1972 and passed into private ownership c1990. ∎

Driver's view of the magnificent
Forth Bridge, probably the best
known example of railway
infrastructure in the world. It was
the world's first major steel bridge
and is 1.5 miles long. Completed
in March 1890 there were 54,000
tons of steel and 6,500,000 rivets
used in its construction. The
building work during its most
intensive stages entailed the
employment of 4000 men of
which 57 sadly lost their lives.
John Griffith

Left: **Seen leaving the bridge is the North British Railway-built Reid J37 0-6-0 64559 which entered service in 1918 and served BR until 1963. The J37s were the most powerful 0-6-0 locomotives built for a Scottish Railway; they were classified 5F by BR.**

Below: **In the same location is Gresley V3 2-6-2T 3MT 67608, which was converted from V1 by BR in 1953, coming off the Forth Bridge at Dalmeny Station.**
Both pictures David Anderson.

Above: **Gresley A3 4-6-2 7P 60073 'St. Gatien', which was in BR service until October 1963, is pictured 'light engine' passing Princes Street Gardens, Edinburgh.**

Left: **Ex-LNER Peppercorn 7MT A2 4-6-2 60537 'Bachelors Button', which entered BR service in June 1948, is seen passing Haymarket Shed (64B) with a 'Down' North Briton.**
Both pictures David Anderson.

Right: **Derby-built Stanier 5MT 4-6-0 45497 is pictured having run around its train and waiting to depart from Kyle of Lochalsh.**

Below: **Seen passing Dalry Road shed (64C) is Crewe-built Stanier Jubilee 4-6-0 45691 'Orion' which served BR until December 1962.**
Both pictures David Anderson.

Above: **Ex-NBR C16 Class 4-4-2T 67494 looks in splendid condition for a 1916-built engine. Seen heading away from Polmont with a two-coach passenger service to Falkirk and Grangemouth.**

Left: **A delightful scene on the Killin Branch Line (closed 1965). Pictured is 55222 a 1900-built McIntosh ex-Caledonian 2P 0-4-4T.**
Both pictures David Anderson.

Right: **Overgrown and under used Moffat Station which closed to passengers in 1964 and to all traffic 10 years later. Ex-Caledonian 2P 0-4-4T 55164 is seen with a brake van after shunting the soon-to-be closed Beattock-Moffat Branch Line.**

Below: **Travelling the Edinburgh South Side Suburban Line with a train of loose coupled empties is an ancient but nevertheless delightful Drummond Caledonian 2F 0-6-0. Number 57287 was built at St Rollox works and entered service in September 1896; the loco was withdrawn by BR in November 1961.**
Both pictures David Anderson.

Above: **Preserved Stanier 8F 2-8-0 seen in action at the Severn Valley Railway. An engine which went to war and then returned to the UK, it was LMS 8233, WD307, Iran Railways 41-109, WD 70307 and then WD500 and eventually 48773.**

Left: **Stanier 2-8-0 48722 is pictured thundering through Delamere Forest on the former Cheshire Lines in June 1967. This Brighton-built loco lasted in BR service until May 1968, almost to the end of steam.**

THE ULTIMATE FREIGHT
LOCOMOTIVE
The Stanier Class 8F 2-8-0

When in the 1930s the LMS were faced with more freight traffic than they had reliable locomotives to handle it with, a brilliant William A Stanier design provided the solution. The 2-8-0 8F was a success story right from the moment that the first example 48000 (LMS number 8000) rolled out of Crewe Works in June 1935. But the 8F story is not just a Crewe story as 849 of the type were built all over the United Kingdom. BR number sequence 48000 to 48775.

Stanier had taken the experience gained in the construction of his highly successful 'Black Five' class and applied those criteria in a scaled-up form to his new freight locomotive. The 8Fs, in addition to fulfilling freight duties, rode well at speed and were widely used on passenger trains, running at speeds of up to 60mph. They steamed well, had spacious cabs, and were reliable, all features which made them nationally acceptable to crews and depot managers.

The Second World War saw the 8Fs pressed into intensive service not only at home but also overseas; the class staked its claim to be known as Britain's 'engine of war'. The wartime Government ordered that 208 of the engines be constructed by Beyer Peacock and the North British Locomotive Company, and requisitioned a further 51 from the LMS, shipping the whole batch overseas. Several were lost at sea aboard torpedoed ships but the majority made it to the Middle East where, after being converted to oil burners, served on vital supply routes. Some stayed overseas and worked for several years after the war, those combined with the war damaged or lost locomotives account for the difference in 'build' and 'taken into BR stock' figures.

BR originally operated 663 of the class, and a further three were returned from the military in 1957 making that total 666. Locomotive No 48616 became the first to be scrapped following a derailment in 1960 and withdrawals proper began with No 48009 leading the way to the scrap yards in December 1962, but approximately 150 examples survived into the last years of BR steam. Eight of the class have been preserved.

The complex WD histories of some of the type can be appreciated by looking at the timeline of preserved locomotive No 48773 (SVR). It was built by North British (works number 24607) and entered LMS service as 8233 in 1940. In 1941 it became WD 307 and was sent overseas where it became 41-109 of Iran State Railways; in 1952 it returned to the UK as WD 70307. It was then refurbished at Derby and resumed military service in the UK as WD 500. In 1957 it came back into BR stock and first given the number 90733, which was later changed to 48773.

Below: **Working hard! Stanier 8F 2-8-0 48642, seen near Kilnhurst in this 1950s picture. This loco served BR until 1964.**

BUILD TOTALS OF THE **STANIER 'CLASS 8F' 2-8-0:**		
North British Locomotive Co 208, Crewe 136, Brighton 93, Swindon 80, Horwich 75, Vulcan Foundry 67, Darlington 53, Doncaster 50, Beyer Peacock 50, Eastleigh 23, Ashford 14.		

Above: **Clanking through Tiviot Dale in 1967, Crewe-built Stanier 8F 2-8-0 No 48329.**

Right: **Stanier 8F 2-8-0 48702, a Brighton-built example, is pictured travelling tender first through Manchester Victoria Station in the 1960s.**

Left: **December 1965 and 8F 2-8-0 48544 looks to be in good condition, seen at Buxton (then 9L formerly 9D) This was an LNER-built (Darlington) engine which was transferred to the LMS in 1946. Withdrawn by BR March 1968.**

A fantastic free day out

Enjoy action-packed fun for the whole family!

Open daily 10.00-18.00, closed 24-26 December

National Railway Museum
Leeman Road
York
YO26 4XJ
T: 0844 815 3139

www.nrm.org.uk

*We reserve the right to charge admission for special events

BLACK FIVES THE LMS MAIDS OF ALL WORK!

Almost every popular adjective has been applied to descriptions of this class of mixed traffic locomotive with the most appropriate possibly being 'ubiquitous'. Being so numerous a class, 842 built between 1934 and 1951, they really did appear to be everywhere at once and the Stanier Class 5MT 4-6-0s were rightly described as 'maids of all work'. The BR class number sequence was 44658 to 45499.

Black Five 45227 waits to depart from Leeds City in 1963, young enthusiasts join the driver in watching for the 'right away' signal. Note the BR DMU in the opposite platform, a sign of things to come.

During their long working lives (1934 to 1968) they were just as likely to be found on a main line express as busy shunting wagons for a branch line goods train. The real success story of the design undoubtedly stemmed from its route availability as the Black Five's weight and length gave it the freedom to range over almost all of first the LMS system and later elsewhere.

This new-build design was urgently needed by the LMS and, accordingly, the first batch was also ordered straight off the drawing board without a prototype engine being trialled. These tapered boiler two-cylinder sleek-looking locomotives were a success right from the start. Modifications to the type were, of course, made as production began, but the basic design had proved to be sound and the locos were almost universally popular with footplate and maintenance crews. The first of the class to enter LMS service was 5020 (BR No 45020) which left the works of Vulcan Foundry, Newton-le-Willows, in August 1934.

British Steam

Above: **Seen in LMS guise, Black Five No 5000 (LMS No 45000) is pictured at the Severn Valley Railway. This loco is preserved as part of the National Collection.**

BUILD TOTALS OF THE STANIER BLACK FIVE 'CLASS 5MT' 4-6-0:

Armstrong Whitworth & Co 327, Crewe 210, Horwich 105, Vulcan Foundry 100, Derby 100.

The record for the largest 'single build order' placed by a railway company concerned 227 engines of this class and was awarded to Armstrong Whitworth & Co. That contract was worth £1,380,160 (£6080 per engine and tender). The manufactured price constantly increased during the 16-year life of the build eg 1943 Crewe-built engines having a sanctioned cost of £9500 each. The 1948 price for Horwich-built examples 44698-44717 was £14,450 each, £20,642 each being the cost of the last two built 44686/7.

HG Ivatt, during his time as CME of the LMS, produced nine experimental variants of the 'Black Five' design. Because of a 'coal crisis' after WWII five engines 44826/7 44829/30 and 44844 were converted to oil burners but all were converted back to coal burners by the end of 1948. While in BR service four of the class carried names, 45154 'Lanarkshire Yeomanry', 45156 'Ayrshire Yeomanry', 45157 'The Glasgow Highlander' and 45158 'Glasgow Yeomanry'.

Withdrawal of the class started in 1961 and No 45401 was the first but, significantly, seven years later on 4 August 1968, it was 'Black Five' No 45212 that had the dubious honour of hauling the last timetabled steam train for British Railways. Stanier described the 'Black Five' as being 'a deuce of a good engine' so he would no doubt have been pleased to know that 18 of the locomotives made it into preservation, the vast majority of which have steamed again. ∎

Stanier 5MT 4-6-0 44687 pictured at Blackpool in 1958. The last of the class to be built, it was completed at Horwich by BR in May 1951. Note the differences, it is fitted with outside Caprotti valve gear and a high running plate on the style of the Ivatt 4MT Moguls, plus a double chimney. This loco was withdrawn in January 1966.

Top: **Seen at Longsight (9A) depot in 1961, 5MT 4-6-0 44751. This loco is another Black Five variant as the rather ungainly front end shows. The engine is fitted with Caprotti valve gear and a low running plate, also fitted with Timken roller bearings. This loco was withdrawn in October 1964.**

Above: **5MT 4-6-0, 44693 leaves Colwyn Bay with a holiday relief train for Crewe 23 August 1958. This was a 1950 Horwich-built engine which was withdrawn in May 1967.**

Left: **Vulcan Foundry-built 5MT 4-6-0, 45101 is seen about to depart from Manchester Victoria in 1957. Withdrawn March 1968.**

Right: **5MT 5-6-0, 45363 working hard on Bentham Bank in July 1963. This loco was withdrawn in October 1967.**

Below: **Named Stanier 5MT 4-6-0, 45156 'Ayrshire Yeomanry' is pictured at Fleetwood on 20 April 1968 with an excursion. This Armstrong Whitworth-built loco lasted until the end of BR steam, it was cut up in December 1968.**

Bottom: **5MT 4-6-0, 44727 is seen at Ribblehead Station on the Settle-Carlisle route in 1965. This was one of 10 Crewe 1949-built engines constructed with steel fireboxes (44718-44727).**

North British Locomotive Co Ltd of Glasgow-built Thompson B1 5MT 4-6-0, 61264. This loco entered BR service in December 1947, withdrawn in December 1965. Pictured at the Churnet Valley Railway, it is one of two preserved examples.

B1
THOMPSON'S FINEST

The B1 mixed traffic locomotive was designer Edward Thompson's first for the LNER; the 4-6-0 was universally acclaimed as being his finest work. Edward Thompson became CME of the London North Eastern Railway at the age of 59, succeeding Sir Nigel Gresley in 1941. Reportedly there was 'history' between Thompson and his illustrious predecessor; to put it mildly Thompson had other 'loyalties' at the time of the formation of the LNER.

Gresley, who became the first LNER Chief Mechanical Engineer (1923-41), was ex-Great Northern Railway and he got the post in preference to Sir Vincent Raven ex-North Eastern Railway. The appointment apparently did not sit well with Thompson who thought that his former NER colleague was the better man for the job. As for the loyalties, ex-NER engineer Thompson was Vincent Raven's son-in-law!

Thompson was only appointed after the LNER Chairman Sir Ronald Matthews failed in two unsuccessful head-hunting missions. When Gresley intimated an earlier than expected retirement, because of poor health, it gave the LNER a

problem as no member of staff had been identified as his successor! Firstly Matthews tried to tempt Oliver Bulleid back from the SR (whom he had joined in 1937); 'OB' was engaged in the development of his new 'Merchant Navy Pacific' and refused a move back to Doncaster.

The chairman's next target was Roland C Bond of the LMS, but he had just been put in charge of the workshops at Crewe and also declined the move. Gresley died on 5 April 1941 and there being no other candidates Edward Thompson was appointed CME of the LNER on 24 April 1941. He served until 1946, when he was succeeded by Arthur Peppercorn who became the last CME of the LNER.

Above: **Thompson B1 5MT 4-6-0, 61397 is one of the last NBL-built engines outshopped in March 1952; a Scottish B1 this loco's home shed was St Margaret's (64A). This locomotive has electric lights (note the turbo generator on running board) and in addition the smokebox number plate is higher than normal (above the top door hinge) there is also an extra footstep welded onto the right-hand bottom section of the smokebox door. The B1 is pictured working hard between Inverkeithing and North Queensferry on a southbound freight.**
David Anderson.

B1 4-6-0, 61058, a NBL 1946 loco, is seen running forward in order to gain the nearside line and then set back to couple up to the waiting stock; 61058 was cut up in June 1966. This picture was taken in 1959 at Sheffield Victoria Station which closed to all traffic on 5 January 1970. The overhead wires seen are those of the 1500V DC Woodhead Route,

BUILD TOTALS 'B1 CLASS' 4-6-0 5MT		
Darlington	1942/47	60 locos
		(3 batches)
Gorton	1948/49	10 locos
North British Locomotive Co Ltd	1946/52	290 locos
		(3 batches)
Vulcan Foundry Ltd	1947	50 locos

Below: **Preserved B1 61264 looking resplendent with LNER livery and number.**

The success of Thompson's 'B1' 4-6-0 5MT locomotives and the 'L1 Class' 2-6-4Ts which followed more than justified his appointment as CME. The B1s were intended to replace various 'tired' 4-4-2, 4-4-0 and 4-6-0 types which the LNER inherited at the time of 'Amalgamation'. To provide a good mixed traffic locomotive with wide route availability Thompson opted for a two-cylinder design with easier to maintain Walschaert piston valves, that is, in comparison to the difficult to maintain conjugated valve gear used by Gresley on his LNER three-cylinder locos.

So difficult were the post-war working conditions that it took almost two years for the first 10 new engines to be built. The first B1 4-6-0, 61000 'Springbok' emerged from Darlington Works in December 1942, with the tenth 61009 'Hartebeeste' following in April 1944. The B1s compared favourably with the LMS 'Black Fives' and GWR 'Halls' and they became popular engines working all over the ex-LNER routes of the new BR regions.

Between 1942 and 1952 a total of 410 B1s were built, numbers 61000-61273 by the LNER, and 61274-61409 by British Railways. The first 40 engines were named after different types of antelope and when those options ran out a further 18 were named after LNER directors, in addition 61379 was named 'Mayflower', however the majority of the class remained un-named. On 7 March 1950, No 61057 crashed into a goods train in dense fog; the engine was scrapped due to the severe nature of the damage. Accordingly the highest number of B1s in service was 409. ∎

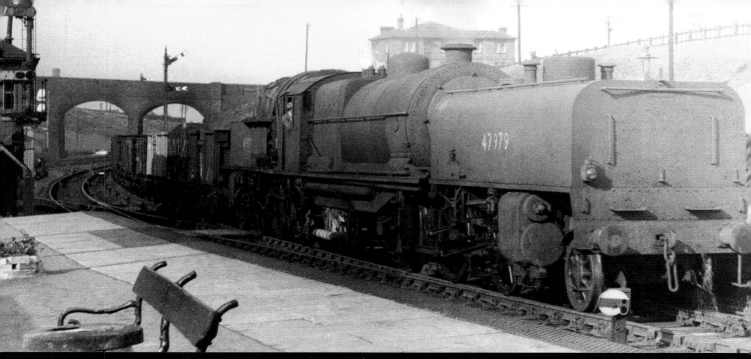

FREIGHT ICON – BEYER GARRATT

It is almost impossible to confuse the Beyer Garratt type of steam locomotive with any other design. Produced in the UK by Beyer Peacock of Manchester they were essentially two locomotives in one. The type found great favour with railways worldwide and were built to various gauges but on the UK standard gauge only small numbers were employed, one locomotive by the LNER and 33 locomotives by the LMS. All 34 passed into BR ownership but their reign was to be a short one due mainly to excessive maintenance costs and high fuel consumption. By April 1958 all had been withdrawn from service.

The LNER locomotive was known as the 'U1' Gresley Beyer Garratt and was the result of collaboration between the LNER CME and Beyer Peacock Ltd. It entered service in June 1925 and carried the LNER number 9999, which became BR number 69999. It was the most powerful locomotive ever put to work in the UK and was built with a 2-8-0 + 0-8-2 wheel arrangement making it a 2-8-8-2T ('T' because Garratts are tank locos), in essence it was two 2-8-0 engines.

The powerful six-cylinder locomotive was built to bank 700-ton trains over the Worsborough Incline, which included three miles at a gradient of 1-in-40.

Under BR the ex-LMS Garratts were serviced at Crewe Works. Locomotive 47998 (with open tender) is pictured during an April 1955 visit. This locomotive was withdrawn by BR from Toton MPD (18A) in August 1956 and cut up at Crewe in October.

When that line was electrified the loco was transferred to the Lickey Incline but in that employ the large grate area proved too much for one fireman to handle and so 69999 was converted to an oil burner in 1955. Nevertheless BR took the 'U1' out of service in December of that year, and cut it up three months later.

The LMS Fowler Beyer Garratts were smaller and less powerful locomotives than the 'U1' and had the same wheel arrangement and cylinder size as the Horwich-built 'Crabs'. They had a 2-6-0 + 0-6-2 wheel arrangement making them 2-6-6-2Ts, and effectively two 2-6-0 engines. The LMS bought three of the type from Beyer Peacock in March 1927 and a further 30 in 1930. The class carried the LMS numbers 7967-7999 and from 1948 the British Railways numbers 47967-47999.

In 1931 all but two of the class (47998 and 47999) were fitted with revolving coal bunkers driven by a two-cylinder auxiliary steam engine. The LMS Garratts worked heavy coal trains between Toton and Brent alleviating the need for double heading. They were kept in service into the mid-1950s but withdrawal of the class started in the summer of 1955. No BR Garratts were preserved.

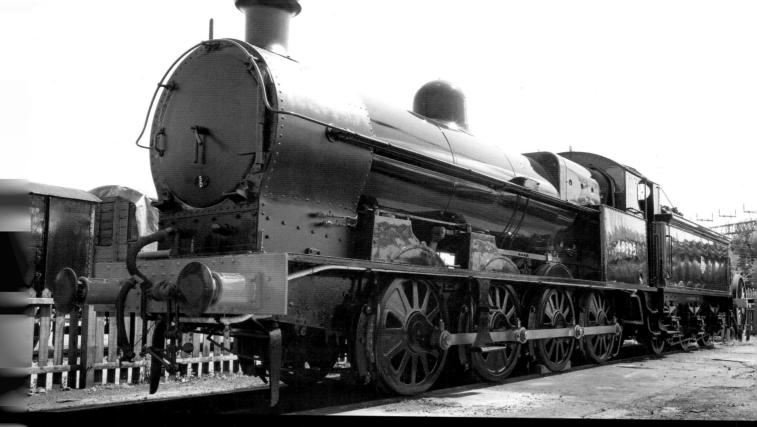

FREIGHT ICON – SUPER D

The original 'G' Class' LNWR 0-8-0 6F goods engines were introduced prior to 1912 by Francis W Webb and George Whale for the LNWR and were built at Crewe Works. In 1912 Charles Bowen-Cooke (CME at Crewe Works 1909/20) commenced fitting superheated boilers to the locomotive type, thus the name 'Super D' entered locomotive building history.

Thereafter the design was refined by Bowen-Cooke's successor Capt Hewitt Pearson Montague Beames (1921/22) who introduced a 'G2 Class' variant and also a 'G2A' locomotive, both with higher capacity boilers, which earned them a power rating of 7F. Between 1929 and 1932 a batch of 175 superheated locomotives were built by Sir Henry Fowler as a development of the G2 type, for the then London Midland & Scottish Railway. But colloquially all of the variants were simply referred to as Bowen-Cooke Super Ds.

The name 'Super D' is a title worthy of explanation. The term first referred to the original Bowen-Cooke G1 types; they were rebuilds of earlier Francis W Webb LNWR engines. At that period in time, locomen commonly called every 0-8-0 engine with a large boiler a 'D'. After 1912, the Bowen-Cooke practice of using superheating in boiler design gave rise to the term 'Super', hence these distinctive-looking LNWR 0-8-0s became known as 'Super Ds'.

The superheating principle involves passing the saturated steam through a series of heater elements situated in the boiler's large flue tubes. Early superheaters were fitted in the smokebox, and were little more than steam dryers. Later superheaters used enlarged boiler tubes to dry the steam and raise the temperature to a higher level. The resultant 'superheated steam' when fed to the cylinders is hotter, drier, and as a result, has greater expansive qualities, thus

producing more power. Superheating can lead to savings of 25 per cent in coal and 30 per cent in water consumption.

The 'Super D' 0-8-0s earned the reputation of being vocal locomotives and they could be heard miles away with their 'two-loud-then-two-gentle' exhaust beats, with the second of the loud beats being noticeably louder than the first. In addition, the distinctive wheeze attributed to the type of 'Joy' valve gear used on these engines, in conjunction with the constant ringing of the side rods, made them audibly unique.

The combined class gave great service and, although withdrawal from traffic started in 1947, several engines earned a reprieve and were, in fact, given heavy overhauls owing to a shortage of freight engines post-WWII. Transferred into BR ownership in 1948 were 509 locos made up of 121 G1 type, 60 G2 type and 328 G2A classes, however seven of the G2As were allocated BR numbers but were scrapped before receiving them. One locomotive survived into preservation and that example is number 49395; it is a G2 type, built at Crewe in 1921 and retired from Buxton (9D) depot in November 1959; it is part of the national collection.

Top: **Preserved LNWR 'Super D' 0-8-0 49395 pictured after the completion of its rebuild by L&NWR Heritage Company Ltd Crewe. LNWR engines in general and the Super Ds in particular did not carry a number on the smokebox, both the LMS and BR continued that practice.**

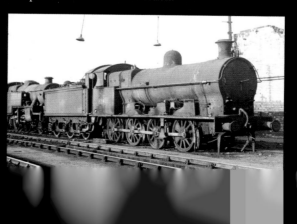

Left: **Seen at Gorton (39A) in March 1961 is G2 type 'Super D' 49421. This loco entered service in March 1922 and was withdrawn by BR in October 1961.**

BRITISH RAILWAYS 0-6-0s

British Railways inherited a multiplicity of steam locomotives from the 'Big four' railway companies and included in the stock lists were over 50 classes of 'six-coupled' tender locomotives. The actual number of 0-6-0 tender types in the 1948 steam locomotive census was 4210. A fact worthy of note is that 0-6-0T tank engines came a close second with 3010 of those types passing into BR ownership.

Above: **One of the most famous 0-6-0 classes was the LNWR '18-inch Goods'; Crewe Works produced 310 of the 2F tender types between 1880 and 1892, 75 of the 0-6-0s were taken into BR stock. The type were nicknamed 'Cauliflowers' because the LNWR crest originally carried on the centre wheel splasher was thought by locomen to resemble that vegetable. Although built as 'fast' goods engines the class were often to be seen on passenger workings. Six of the class survived into 1955 and one such was 58409 (built October 1900) pictured at Keswick on 15 July 1955; this Webb 0-6-0 was withdrawn by BR in December of that year. The last passenger train ran on the Cockermouth Keswick & Penrith Railway on 4 March 1972.**

BR 0-6-0s varied greatly in type and power rating ranging from the Southern Region's ex-SECR '01 Class' engines, rated at 1F, to the powerful ex-LNER Gresley 'J38 Class', rated at 6F. Oliver Bulleid's unconventional looking 'Q1 Class' rated at 5F, were perhaps the most unusual 0-6-0s taken into BR stock but the accolade for the most numerous class belongs to the ex-Midland Railway/LMS.

The Fowler-designed Midland Railway 4Fs in the BR number series 43835 to 44026 were built between 1911 and 1923 and totalled 192 locomotives. In 1924 a further building programme of the type was embarked upon which concluded in 1940, after 580 locomotives had been built. During that project the 0-6-0s were constructed not only by the LMS works at Derby, Crewe and St Rollox but by contractors Andrew Barclay Sons & Co Ltd and Kerr Stuart & Co Ltd.

EX 'BIG FOUR' TOTALS OF 0-6-0 TYPES TAKEN INTO BR STOCK:	
Great Western Railway	183 locomotives
Southern Railway	312 locomotives
London Midland Scottish Railway	2057 locomotives
London North Eastern Railway	1658 locomotives

Combining the two build totals shows that 772 Fowler 4F 0-6-0 locomotives were taken into BR stock.

Considering that such a large number of 0-6-0s were operated by BR it is interesting to note that none made it through to the last year of steam operation. Statistics show that the type was withdrawn steadily over the 20 years of BR steam, for example the number in service had reduced to 2821 by the end of 1958. Five years later only 545 working 0-6-0s remained and that total was reduced to only 104 in 1965.

A TRIO OF EX-NORTH BRITISH RAILWAY 0-6-0 Js

Above: J35 Pictured at Saughton Junction Edinburgh with a Glasgow-bound freight is Cowlairs-built, Reid-designed, NBR 'B Class', ex-LNER 'J35' 3F 0-6-0 number 64534. This loco was the last in a class of 76 built 1906-1913 and given the LNER numbers 4460 to 4535 (BR 64460-64535). BR inherited only 70 of the class as six engines were scrapped prior to 1948. All 70 locos worked up to 1958 on both freight and secondary passenger duties with some even staying in use up to, but not beyond the end of, 1961. Loco 64534 was withdrawn in November 1961.

Left: J36 Holmes-designed NBR 'C Class', ex-LNER 'J36 Class' 2F 0-6-0 number 65280 is pictured passing Gorgie East on the Edinburgh Suburban Line. Number 65280 was built at Cowlairs Works in 1896 and served NBR, LNER and BR for a total of 66 years. The 'C Class' of 168 engines was North British Railways' most numerous locomotive type, they were given the LNER numbers 5210 to 5346 (BR 65210-65346). BR took into stock 118 examples which by 1958 was reduced to 86 and to only three in 1966, with none surviving the end of steam. One example 65243 'Maude' is preserved.

Right: J37 Another nostalgic scene from the Edinburgh Suburban Line, this time the locomotive is a Reid-designed 0-6-0 number 64597. The 104 NBR 'S Class' superheated locomotives were built between 1914 and 1921 at Cowlairs Works and North British Locomotive Co Ltd. When built they were the most powerful 0-6-0s ever to be built for use on any Scottish railway. They were taken into BR stock with a 4F power rating but were uprated to 5F in 1953. The class carried LNER numbers 4536 to 4639 (BR 64536-64639). In 1958 BR were still operating 101 of the class, four of which survived beyond the end of 1966, but none to the end of steam. NBL-built example 64597 was withdrawn by BR in August 1966.

TITLED TRAINS

Above: **West Country Class Bullied Pacific 34092 'City of Wells' is pictured at Barford St Martin, during a preserved era run between Salisbury and Yeovil Junction. The loco is carrying the celebrated 'Golden Arrow' insignia on its smokebox door and boiler, plus the traditional flags. In its heyday the famous boat train departed from London's Victoria Station at 10am and was timed to arrive in Dover just 100 minutes later! That was achieved with a typical load of 10 Pullman cars plus two baggage cars.**
Brian Sharpe.

The naming of trains was a tradition almost as old as the railways themselves. Many of the names were equally familiar to both enthusiasts and members of the public; so much so that they are still remembered some 40 years after they ceased to operate. Name boards on the front of the locomotives hauling such trains were commonplace, but it must be remembered that towards the end of BR operations not all of the network's named trains always carried them.

On 'Big four' and BR corridor stock titled trains during the steam era it was not uncommon for door-sized 'tail boards' to be affixed as a blank to the corridor connection of the train's trailing coach. In 1946 the distinguished railway writer CJ Allen compiled a list of over 130 regularly timetabled titled trains; in the early days of British Railways around 80 of those services could still be seen around the regions. In addition many trains (not just those with titles) carried destination boards on their carriages.

Among the most famous names were Flying Scotsman (King's Cross-Waverley), the Silver Jubilee (King's Cross-Newcastle Central), The Elizabethan (King's Cross-Waverley), The Irish Mail (Euston-Holyhead), Coronation Scot (Euston-Glasgow Central), Royal Scot (Euston-Glasgow Central), the Cheltenham Flyer (Paddington-Cheltenham), the Bristolian (Paddington-Bristol), the Cornish Riviera (Paddington-Plymouth), the Brighton Belle (Victoria-Brighton) and of course the illustrious Golden Arrow (Victoria-Dover). There were many more and all equally worthy of mention which, sadly, available space does not permit.

Above: **Locomotive change at Leeds City in August 1958. Nottingham-based Stanier Jubilee 4-6-0, 45650 'Blake' is seen before setting back onto the stock of 'The Waverley'. 'The Waverley' name was carried by the 9.15am St Pancras-Edinburgh Waverley service post-WWII. The route was via Nottingham, Leeds, and Carlisle. Edinburgh was gained via the Waverley Route.**

Left: **Ex-GWR Modified Hall Class 4-6-0, 7929 'Wyke Hall' is pictured departing Torquay in 1959 with 'The Devonian'. This was often a heavily loaded train which operated between Bradford Forster Square and Paignton via Leeds, Birmingham New Street and Bristol Temple Meads.**

Right: **British Railways decided to give the more prominent boat trains to Southampton Docks special names, one such was the 'Union Castle Express', running from London Waterloo. The special boat train connected with the Union-Castle Line express mailships to South Africa which sailed from Southampton Western Docks. Unrebuilt Bullied Pacific 34013 'Okehampton' is seen passing Raynes Park on Union Castle duty.**

Above: **BR-built GWR Manor 7828 'Odney Manor', the 4-6-0 is pictured in 1963 waiting to depart Shrewsbury for the Cambrian coast hauling the final leg of the down London Paddington-Aberystwyth 'Cambrian Coast Express'. The train arrived at Shrewsbury via Birmingham Snow Hill and Wolverhampton.**

Left: **The prestigious 'Yorkshire Pullman' service ran between London King's Cross and Hull. Ex-LNER A1 4-6-2 60120 'Kittiwake' is seen departing Doncaster with an 'up' service in 1955.**

Right: **The record-breaking Gresley A4 Pacific 60022 'Mallard' is pictured taking water at Doncaster during an August 1957 'down' run of 'The Elizabethan'. This is an unusual occurrence as 'The Elizabethan' was rostered as a non-stop service (both ways) between London King's Cross and Edinburgh Waverley; the impromptu stop may have been because one of the water troughs was temporarily out of action. The non-stop service was renamed to commemorate the coronation of Queen Elizabeth II in 1953; it was formerly called the 'Capitals Limited'.**

Above: **71000 'Duke of Gloucester' is pictured having just arrived at Crewe with the down 'Mid-Day Scot' on 1 June 1956; the unique Riddles 8P Pacific is attracting the attention of a group of schoolboy 'spotters'. The Standard 4-6-2 is about to be uncoupled from the train and go onto the shed. The timings of the 'Mid-Day Scot' at that time were Euston depart 1.30pm, one intermediate stop at Rugby 2.50 to 2.54pm. After a booked engine change the train left Crewe at 4.20pm and with one stop at Carlisle was due at Glasgow Central at 9.10pm. 71000 is a preserved locomotive.** *Peter Kerslake.*

WEST COAST **SCOTS**

Below: **Stanier 8P 4-6-2 46236 'City of Bradford' waits at Crewe to take the 'Mid-Day Scot' north on 1 June 1956, in fact taking over from 71000 'Duke of Gloucester'. Behind the locomotive is the Plymouth 'through coach' which would have left the South West at 8am as part of a Plymouth-Liverpool/Manchester service, arriving in Crewe at 3.49pm. 'City of Bradford' entered LMS service in July 1939 as a streamlined engine, 46236 served BR (in un-streamlined form) until October 1964, being cut up two months later.** *Peter Kerslake.*

Above: **46253 'City of St Albans' is seen on 9 July 1960 nearing Beattock Summit with the down 'Royal Scot'. Pacific 46253 would have come onto the London Euston-Glasgow Central train at Crewe. The 'Royal Scot' trains left Euston and Glasgow Central respectively at 10am, and both were timed to arrive at their destinations at 5.15pm (Sunday times varied). 'City of St Albans' entered LMS service in September 1946 and was withdrawn by BR in October 1964, and cut up two months later. No Stanier 8P 'Princess Coronation' (Duchess) locomotives worked for BR after 1964. Three examples are preserved, 46229, 46233 and 46235.** *David Anderson.*

In 1972 British Railways were still proudly declaring that the VOR was 'the last steam train on BR'. Loco No 8 'LLYWELYN' is pictured after arriving at Devil's Bridge and preparing to run around its stock. Note the BR Blue of the 'Class 98'.

BRITISH RAILWAYS
NARROW GAUGE

When British Railways decreed that 8 August 1968 would be their last day of steam operation they did not include in that moratorium a magical bit of ex-GWR territory in the west of Wales.

In this 1968 shot No 8 is seen taking water just outside the station at Devil's Bridge.
Roger Jermy.

The Vale of Rheidol narrow gauge railway operating between Aberystwyth and Devil's Bridge was taken into Cambrian Railway ownership in 1913, GWR ownership in 1923 and BR ownership in 1948. After 1968 the remaining three steam locomotives on the route continued to operate under BR for another 21 years before finally ceasing to be BR stock in 1989.

They were also the only steam locomotives to carry the new 'BR Blue' livery when post-1968 they became BR 'Class 98'. The 1ft 11½in gauge railway was finally sold to the Brecon Mountain Railway as a going concern, and they were still operating the historic route as the new millennium dawned. The locomotives are all GWR Swindon-built 2-6-2Ts built in 1923/24 to replace the original ex-Cambrian locomotives inherited by the GWR. The engines are No 7 'OWAIN GLYNDWR', No 8 'LLYWELYN' and No 9 'PRINCE OF WALES'.

The Vale of Rheidol engines were not the only narrow gauge stock to come into BR ownership on 1 January 1948.

The Vale of Rheidol engines were not the only narrow gauge stock to come into BR ownership on 1 January 1948. There were two Welshpool & Llanfair Railway 2ft 6in gauge 0-6-0T locomotives which BR took out of service in 1961; after being stored for two years they were then acquired by the Welshpool & Llanfair Light Railway Preservation Company in 1963. Additionally two Corris Railway 2ft 3in gauge 0-4-2ST locomotives came into BR ownership at the time of nationalisation but were disposed of in October 1948, after a flood cut the river Dovey bridge marooning them in Machynlleth. In May 1951 they passed into Tal-y-Llyn Railway ownership. ■

Above: **Class '98' 2-4-2T 'OWAIN GLYNDWR' waits to get away from Aberystwyth.**

Left: **The VOR in new safe hands. Loco No 7 'OWAIN GLYNDWR' is seen making its way up to Devil's Bridge in spring sunshine, 1991.**

Right: **Devil's Bridge (Pontarfynach) after BR. No 7 and train arriving in summer sunshine.**

WHEEL ARRANGEMENTS
As applied to British steam locomotives

There is no mystery in the wheel arrangement annotations given to locomotives; the system is easy to understand and simply helps to identify an engine type. For those seeking wider knowledge the wheel arrangement is sometimes a good indicator of the type of work the locomotive has been designed to do.

Standard 9F 92027 with one leading wheel on each side, five main (driving wheels) and no wheel under the cab illustrates the 2-10-0 configuration.

A SELECTION OF THE COMMON WHEEL ARRANGEMENTS USED FROM 1923 ONWARDS:

- 4-4-0 American
- 4-4-2 Atlantic
- 0-6-0
- 2-6-0 Mogul
- 2-6-2 Prairie
- 2-6-4 Adriatic
- 4-6-0 Ten-wheeler
- 4-6-2 Pacific
- 4-6-4 Hudson, Baltic
- 0-8-0
- 2-8-0 Consolidation
- 2-8-2 Mikado
- 4-8-0

The way that British locomotive wheel arrangements are described is taken from a system developed by the US Engineer Frederic Whyte. The Whyte system counts the wheels, and shows three numbers which are separated by dashes. The first number gives the leading/carrying wheels, the second number refers to the driving wheels and the third number applies to the rear carrying wheels. The letter T after combination denotes that it refers to a tank engine (ie a locomotive without a separate tender). The wheels on any tender attached to a locomotive form no part of the wheel arrangement notation. The two parts of an articulated locomotive are described separately and joined by a + sign.

Given the nationality of this system's originator it is no surprise that the majority of the wheel arrangement names given have their roots in American railway history.

The Adriatic type was first introduced in 1909 and is said to have been derived from an Austrian-built locomotive intended for use on routes bordering the eastern shoreline of that sea. Two sources are offered for the Atlantic type, either Philadelphia Railroad locomotives running out of Atlantic City NJ or taken from a type supplied to the Atlantic Coast Railroad, c1898.

The Consolidation type is thought to have originated from an American loco type favoured at the time of the amalgamation of two railroads in the Lehigh Valley c1865. While the Mikado type is derived from an American design supplied to Japanese Railways in 1897. The Mogul type was first built in 1858 by the US-based Baldwyn Locomotive Works. The same locomotive builders were also responsible for the name Pacific, chosen after they built a batch of locomotives with that configuration for New Zealand Railways. The Prairie type was introduced c1885 and was popularised in the American Midwest.

British Steam

Above: Standard Class 4MT 80022 with (on each side) one leading wheel, three main (driving wheels) and two wheels under the cab and tender illustrates the 2-6-4 configuration.

Below: 7714 ex-GWR 5700 Class 'Pannier Tank' has only the three main wheels (on each side) and thus illustrates the 0-6-0PT configuration.

ON THE SCRAP HEAP!

Top: **Awaiting the cutter's torch, redundant steam locomotives pictured at Woodham Bros, Barry Island, South Wales in 1971.**

August 1968 saw the end of steam haulage on British Railways with Black Five 45212 hauling the last timetabled steam train on 4 August, the official last day being 8 August and four locos (45110, 70013, 44781 and 44871) then rostered for stages of the 315-mile farewell to steam 'Fifteen Guinea Special' (Liverpool-Carlisle-Liverpool) on Sunday 11 August. However the demise of steam traction had been under way for some time prior to that. Over the first 20 years of their existence BW systematically reduced their dependence on steam locomotives even though they continued to introduce them in their first years of operation. During the period BR locomotive works, in addition to several scrap metal contractors, had been actively cutting up redundant steam engines. The reduction in steam locomotive numbers for all regions of BR from 1948 to 1959 was gradual with an average reduction of 500 a year in the number of steam locos at work. The numbers of locos scrapped varied widely from region to region and the chart shows the numbers of engines left in use at the end of each year from 1960 to 1967.

The biggest annual drop in steam locomotive numbers was between 1961 and 1962 when 2923 were withdrawn. The BR steam stock opening figure for 1968 included two B1s being used as stationary boilers and three narrow gauge engines. That stock comprised of 184 locomotives of the 4-6-0 type, 18 locomotives of the 2-10-0 type, and 150 locomotives of the 2-8-0 type. The redundant locomotives which were sent to outside contractors were not all 'cut' straight away and locomotives rescued from those scrap yards formed the nucleus of Britain's preserved steam locomotive fleet. But that, as they say, is another story!

Year end	1960	1961	1962	1963	1964	1965	1966	1967
Ex-BR type	1754	1751	1642	1543	1323	881	494	52
Ex-GWR type	2613	2437	1834	1276	585	35	3	3
Ex-SR type	908	682	477	335	161	109	66	0
Ex-LMS type	5155	4513	3567	3060	2340	1674	1024	307
Ex-LNER type	2866	2325	1265	860	581	304	111	2
Total	13,296	11,708	8785	7074	4990	3003	1698	364

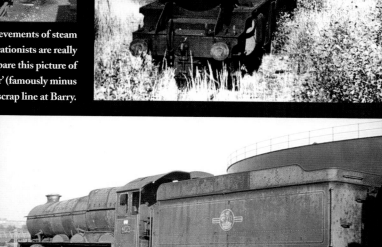

Above: **Some locomotives were in much better condition than others when sent for scrapping Ivatt 2-6-2, 41312 was a late arrival at Barry (circa July 1967) and was rescued and restored to working order. Bullied Pacific Merchant Navy Class 35011 'General Steam Navigation' was also rescued but was still awaiting a return to working order in 2008.**

Left: **This line of discarded steam locomotives make a forlorn sight lined up alongside the main line at Stockport awaiting removal.**

Above: **The fantastic achievements of steam locomotive preservationists are really appreciated when you compare this picture of 71000 'Duke of Gloucester' (famously minus cylinder castings) in the scrap line at Barry.**

Right: **Ex-GWR King 6023 'King Edward II' made it out of Woodham's yard and is now restored. It is pictured in November 1971**

Above: **North British-built LNER B1 4-6-0, 61264 also made it out of the scrap line, where it was pictured in 1970. It can be seen as restored in the 'B1' chapter of this publication**